Down To Earth Cookbook

POLLINATOR PRESS

P.O. Box 78351
San Francisco, CA 94107

www.pollinatorpress.com

Copyright © Lacey Sher and Gail Doherty

All rights reserved. No part of this book may be reproduced or utilized in any form or by any means, electronic or mechanical, including phoyocopying, recording, or by any informational storage and retrieval system, without permission in writing from the publisher.

This book is available for special promotions and premiums.
For details contact Pollinator Press.

First Edition 2006
Printed in the United States of America
10 9 8 7 6 5 4 3 2 1
ISBN 0-9774410-0-9

All photographs by Bob McKay and Elisabeth Koch McKay
www.mckayimaging.com

Front cover logo illustration by Wendy Born Hollander
www.theispot.com/artist/whollander

Book design and layout by Fran Waldmann

Cover design and additional layout by Jason Silverio

Happy Cooking = Healthy Eating!

Contents

Introduction 1
How They Met 3
Why Organic?   Why Vegan?   Why Whole Foods? 4
Basic Kitchen Equipment 7
    SOME TECHNIQUE STUFF 9
    KITCHEN TIPS 10
Pantry 11
Conversion Ideas 19
Spice Blends 20
Basics & Sides 21
    Cooking Beans 22
    Cooking Grains 23
    Vegetable Stock 24
    Almond Milk 25
    Baked Tofu 26
    Basic Marinade 26
    Homemade Seitan 27
    Marinated Tempeh 28
    Caramelized Onions / Caramelized Leeks 29
    Cashew Rice 29
    Bread Sticks 30
    Cornbread 31
    House Marinara 32
    Mushroom Gravy 33
    Peanut Sauce 34
    Nutro Cheese 35
    Sprinkle "Cheese" 36
    Tofu Cheese 36
    Tofu Sour Cream 37
    Mashed Potatoes 38
    Mashed Coconut Yams 39
    Roasted Yams 39
    Cajun Spiced Baked Potato Fries 40
    Sesame Yams 41
    Sauteed Greens 42
    Pickled Vegetables 43

Appetizers ... 45
- Collard Rolls Stuffed with Quinoa, Sweet Potato and Caramelized Onions ... 46
- Cornmeal Cakes with Pico de Gallo ... 47
- Creamy Chickpea Hummus & Oatmeal Garlic Crackers ... 48
- Crispy Wonton Packages ... 49
- Grilled Zucchini Rollatini with Sun-dried Tomatoes and Olives ... 50
- Marinated Stuffed Mushrooms with Tempeh Sausage and Garlic Aioli ... 51
- Pan Grilled Mushroom Tapenade ... 52
- Potato Skins ... 53
- Radiance's Fried Polenta Appetizer ... 54
- Scallion Pancakes with Plum and Dipping Sauces ... 55
- Tofu Hot Wings ... 56
- Tortilla Torte with Creamy Pumpkin Seed Pesto ... 57
- Zucchini Pecan Mini Pancakes ... 58

Soups ... 59
- Black Bean Soup ... 60
- Coconut Squash Soup ... 61
- Curried Red Lentil Soup ... 62
- Gazpacho ... 63
- Mediterranean Lentil Soup ... 64
- Potato Leek Soup with Lemon and Dill ... 65
- Three Bean Chili ... 66
- Quinoa Vegetable Soup ... 67
- Split Pea Soup ... 68
- Sweet Potato Tomato Chipotle Soup ... 69
- Thai Veggie Soup ... 70

Salads ... 71
- Maple Miso Dressing ... 72
- Tangy Tahini Dressing ... 72
- Fennel Apple Dressing ... 73
- Avocado Ranch Dressing ... 73
- Spicy French Dressing ... 74
- Smokey Toasted Sesame Dressing ... 74
- Fresh Herb Vinaigrette ... 75
- Croutons ... 75

Chickpea Untuna Salad 76
Cole Slaw 77
Dark Green Salad 78
Eggless Tofu Salad 79
Gado Gado 80
   Photo page 128
Greek Salad 81
Quinoa Salad 82
Soba Noodles in Peanut Sauce 83
Sea Caesar / Cruelty Free Caesar 84
Hijiki Caviar 85
Spinach Salad with Roasted Balsamic Beets and Spiced Pecans 86
Tofu Nuggets 87
Roasted Tomato, Basil and Corn Salad 88

Sandwiches and Wraps 89

BBQ Tofu Wrap 90
Barbeque Sauce 91
Broccoli Seitan Knishes 92
Club Sandwich 93
Earth Burger 94
Philly Seitan Sandwich 95
Falafel 96
Tahini Sauce 97
Cucumber Salad 97
Gyros 98
Gyro Bread 99
Quinoa Avocado Wrap with Orange Baked Tofu 100
Tofu Parmesan Sandwich 101
Wheatball Sub (a.k.a Wheatball Hoagie, Wheatball Grinder, Wheatball Hero)102

Live Foods 103

Adam's Pink Lady Apple Salsa 104
Curried Almond Pâté 105
Flax Crackers 106
Leaf Wraps 107
   Photo page 125
Sun-Dried Tomato Pâté 107

Live Lasagna	108
Raw Cashew Cheese	109
Live Tomato Sauce	109
Live Nachos	110
Live Pizza Crackers	111
Photo page	*124*
Live Salsa	112
Raw Cheese Trio	113
Raw Herb Vegetable Croquette	114
Raw Cashew Aioli	115
Raw Maki Hand Roll	116
Photo page	*124*
Live Buckwheat Hemp seed Granola Crunch	117
Bliss Cup	118
Nell's Coconut Rolls	119
Raw Apple Pie	120
Raw Cream Whip Topping	121
Raw Lemon Pie	122

Entrées 131

Blue Corn Hempeh	132
Photo page	*126*
Tomato Pudding	133
Chickpea Socca	134
Photo page	*123*
Hijiki Sea Cakes	135
Herbed Tofu Loaf with Apple Herb Stuffing and Cranberry Orange Relish	136-137
Kevin's Tofu Murphy	138
Love Bowl	139
Pizza Crust	140
Coconut Seitan	141
Samosas	142-143
Seitan Satay	144
Photo page	*129*
Southern Style Seitan	145
Thai Coconut Tempeh Stix	146
Vegetable Lasagna	147
White Bean Crêpes with Balsamic Grilled Tempeh & Basil Butter	148-149

    Wild Rice Risotto Cakes 105-151

Drinks, Juices & Smoothies 153

    Bugs Bunny 154
    Circulator 154
    Fruit Slushie 154
    Good Ol' Carrot 155
    Immune Booster 155
    Live Lemonade 156
    Maegan's Heartburn Helper 156
    Rootbeer Float 157
        Photo page 129
    Soy Shake 157
    Strawberry Sunrise 158
    Spirulina Rush 158

Breakfast 159

    Apple Crumb Muffins 160
    Banana Bread 161
    Basic Biscuits 162
    Tempeh Sausage and Gravy Biscuits 163
    Cinnamon Buns 164
    French Toast 165
    Adam's Ginger Oat Waffles with Chamomile Pine Nut Cream & Nectarines .166
    Granola 167
    Lemon Blueberry Scones 168
    Michelle's Blueberry Sour Cream Coffee Cake 169
    Papaya Delight 170
    Quiche 171
    Tempeh Bacun 172
    Tiffany's Pancakes 173
    Tofu Scramble 174

Desserts 175

    Hempseed Cookies 176
    Jam Dot Cookies (Peanut Butter and Jam Cookies) 177
    Magic Cookies 178
        Photo page 129
    Maple Pecan Cookies 179

Oatmeal Raisin Cookies	180
Sugar Cookies	181
Ginger Spice Cookies	181
Blondies	182
Brownies	183
Cheesecake	184
Fruit Sauce	185
Pumpkin Cheesecake	186
Chocolate Cake	187
Chocolate Ganache	188
Chocolate Sauce	188
German Chocolate Cake	189
Peanut Butter Chocolate Cake	190
Vanilla Cake	191
Vanilla Frosting	192
Lemon Coconut Cake	193
Rainforest Crunch Cake	194-195
Photo page	*129*
Tiramisu	196
Luscious Chocolate Brownie Hazelnut Mousse Torte	197
Kit's Peach Skillet Cobbler	198

Kid's Food 199

Ants on a Log	201
Blob on a Biscuit	201
Baby's Apricot Apple Purée	201
Baby's Hot Cereals	202
Baby's Puréed Vegetables	202
Fresh Fruit Kabob	203
Seed Sprinkle	203
Super Power Fruit Shake	204
Toddler's Crunchy Salad Mix	204
Trail Mix	205
Play Clay	205

Acknowledgements 207
Resources 211

Introduction

When we opened Down to Earth, our objective was to create a restaurant that would serve the world at large, as well as the vegan community. In the past, eating out with friends has been difficult for vegans. Many restaurants have been late in recognizing that common 'side dishes' and simple appetizers were inherently vegan or easily made so. We wanted to create a place where vegan diners could come regularly, but to which they would also bring their families and friends for special occasions, with no question of whether the food was vegan. Vegan food had a reputation for being bland and boring, and we were out to disprove that. In sharing the food that we ourselves enjoyed, we were delighted that even non-vegetarians showed up and loved what they ate: delicious, high quality food prepared well.

Organic food was a priority, as well, because we have learned that a commitment to organic food helps us realize the true cost of food. Specifically, we knew that this meant that besides the clear benefits in avoiding carcinogenic pesticides or herbicides, it was important for us to support organic farming, which is not subsidized. This means that organic farmers often pay into the system as taxpayers and with agricultural fees, they seldom or never receive the funding that mainstream corporate farmers get. When you buy organic produce, you know the money you spend is supporting the farmer. One of the direct ways we were able to support organic farming was at our local farm market – where long-time New Jersey farmer Ed Lidzbarski still sells his produce, grown in nearby Freehold on Bruce Springsteen's Certified Organic Farm. He, in turn, shared with us a wealth of information, and has given us valued insights into what it takes to be a small family farmer working in a system that is now dominated by huge conglomerates.

Organic agriculture is ancient, and has been practiced throughout the history of cultivating and growing crops. Until almost the middle of the last century, foods were grown using only natural fertilizers and methods. We wanted to honor that great tradition of working with the earth and the seasons. Preparing good organic food was a perfect, daily, meditative way to do that. In working with fresh, flavorful, naturally grown produce, spices, oils, nuts and legumes, we were perpetuating a tradition that goes back to the original chefs of all cultures, who were 100% organic.

Also important to both of us as vegans was to prepare food that was kind to animals. Once we decided to start a restaurant, it was clear we would be dedicated to creating and using animal-free foods.

As we learned more, we realized there was a profound connection between raising and slaughtering animals for 'meat', and growing and cultivating crops with petrochemicals, artificial hormones and pesticides that affect human hormones. We realized that we had a chance to provide an alternative to both of these very toxic industries. Being in the environmentally-aware Jersey Shore area, we knew we would get a lot of support, and people did respond to the idea of sustainable, sensitive choices. Every meal, every day at Down To Earth reflects this commitment, and, in turn, folks who eat at our restaurant have thanked us for a chance to find fresh, clean and delicious foods. Our beliefs also influenced everyday choices, such as using recycled paper towels and other products, and packaging our takeout food in reusable/recyclable materials.

Down to Earth restaurant is located in downtown Red Bank, an hour south of New York City on the Navesink River at the beginning of the Jersey Shore. We knew this part of New Jersey was ready for a different take on vegetarianism. As we expected, being an organic and vegan restaurant in New Jersey has been both a challenge and a joy. When we opened Down to Earth we were the only restaurant serving organic vegan meals in the entire state of New Jersey! It felt great to be pioneers and we spent much of our time finding sources for the ingredients. As more people began to embrace this way of eating, more resources became available.

Our customers range from tattooed teens to Armani-wearing stock traders. We are a small business and run our restaurant with a hands-on approach, tasting and developing all our recipes as a team. Operating a restaurant is not the easiest task and running one in a basement was even harder. We have managed to transport our patrons and ourselves with food and love to a place higher than the ground itself. We have opened many minds and palates to a whole new fresher way of eating, no matter what a person's diet choices were. We challenged ourselves so that when diners sat down at Down To Earth, they would have their horizons expanded, and we're happy to say that we've heard that confirmed time and again from satisfied diners.

Our philosophy about food stems from our deep love for the Earth and animals that share it with us. When we eat, we are filled with appreciation for the wonderful variety and abundance that surrounds us. It is our hope and belief that by choosing an animal-free diet, we are not contributing any unnecessary suffering in animals' lives. We also look at veganism as a way of lessening the huge impact meat production places on the earth's vital resources. To us, the most important ingredient in our food is love, our love for the earth and its bounty and all of its creatures. That love extends to the care with which we prepare and serve our food, and we believe that the people who eat our food experience that energy and intention in every bite.

Lacey Sher & Gail Doherty

How They Met

It seems that Lacey Sher and Gail Doherty were meant to be great friends and business partners, as they were living almost identical lives right next to each other in a small community in New Jersey. They both worked at local health food stores that were only a few miles apart, both were outgoing and enthusiastic about vegetarianism and both dreamed of opening their own restaurant. Both women had also previously resided in vegetarian-friendly communities—Gail having lived in Hawaii, and Lacey growing up in Marin County, California. Their jobs at their respective health food stores were to make sure that their salad bars were stocked with fresh organic produce in addition to all the fixings that hundreds of hungry lunchtime locals relied on every week. Lacey's husband had friends who worked with Gail and would always say to her "You should meet this girl named Gail, you two would get along great..." and the same to Gail "You've got to meet Lacey; she makes awesome food, too..." Soon they were aware of each other, and it's as if their friendship began even before they met. They knew they would like each other. Their paths synced up once more when they both began attending classes at the Natural Gourmet Institute in New York City. Lacey started her training a few months before Gail, so they weren't in the same classes, but each was aware that the other was attending the school.

A few months passed, and both women stayed dedicated to their culinary educations, taking the train from Red Bank into New York three days a week to attend class. One evening, Gail spotted a woman in chef pants running for the 11 p.m. North Jersey Coast Line train leaving Penn Station bound for Red Bank. She caught up to her and asked "Are you Lacey?" Lacey smiled, nodded yes and asked "Are you Gail?" They made the connection and talked as if they'd known each other all their lives. Both dreamt of opening a restaurant, and most importantly, both recognized that central New Jersey was in need of an organic vegan restaurant.

From that evening, they discussed their dreams of opening a restaurant incessantly and passionately on the train rides back and forth to school. Six months after completing the program, they opened Down To Earth to an enthusiastic full house on December 17th, 1999 and have been serving love-filled vegan meals ever since.

Why Organic? Why Vegan? Why Whole Foods?

Why do we use organic ingredients? We think the better question is 'why would anyone accept food grown with harmful chemicals?' Unfortunately, there is so much confusion surrounding the subject that the answer to this question isn't as obvious as it should be. To put it simply, organic foods are grown without the use of synthetic chemicals, additives, fertilizers or pesticides. Using chemicals to grow food has only been a farming technique since the 1920's, sold to farmers as a way to increase yields and profits. Toxic chemicals, such as DDT, were first developed for the war efforts, to defoliate tropical forests in order to kill mosquitoes carrying malaria. Farmers back at home were sold the same chemicals as a way for them also to fight pests, with little thought of their impact on the earth or the quality of the product. The chemicals worked well enough that the farmers got bigger yields, and the public was none the wiser. Other farmers needed to compete, and so chemical farming became widespread. It wasn't until the 1962 book "Silent Spring" by biologist Rachael Carson that the hazards of this practice were first brought to light, along with the term "Organic Farming." In the years following, support for organic foods has been an up-hill battle. Organic foods in grocery stores, if you could find them, were usually more expensive, and often neglected, looking bad next to the conventional, cheaper produce. Thankfully, these days one can find plenty of organic foods, and dedicated people to support them.

Of course, chemicals used in the growing of food wasn't the only problem. The use of chemicals to make and process food was now a major industry. New advances in food science technology, like factory automation and refining of grains, made possible products with long shelf lives and high profits. Out of nowhere, frozen, freeze-dried, instant, de-nurtured, and artificial foods became the norm in the American kitchen. As a busy society, we embraced these foods, trading our health for the allure of quick and easy meals. We choose to cook with whole foods, foods that have all their edible parts intact, such as unadulterated grains, beans, fruits and vegetables. Eating a diet that is primarily whole foods will give your body the nutrients that are missing in refined foods, and are more easily assimilated and digested.

Why did we choose to keep this cookbook free of animal products, or what is known as 'vegan'? Today, the subject has received much attention and the mere mention of 'vegan' or 'vegetarian' will almost always spark a debate. It is easy to get defensive about the eating of animals on both sides of the argument; the very nature of the question seemingly forces one to choose a side. Religion, history, educated and non-educated opinion and misinformation all complicate the issue. Unfortunately, most people will automatically assume that if you are vegan, you think that those who are not are bad people. Screaming matches between 'militant vegans' and 'angry meat-eaters' make it harder for the truth about the harmful practices of the raising of livestock to come to light. For the same reasons that organic, whole foods are better for you and the earth, so is choosing vegan food. Modern day agriculture's dependence on higher yields accelerates topsoil erosion on our farmlands, rendering land less productive for crop cultivation, and forcing the conversion of wilderness to grazing and farm lands. Animal waste from massive feedlots and factory farms is a leading cause of pollution in our groundwater and rivers. The United Nations Food and Agriculture Organization has linked animal agriculture to a number of other environmental problems, including: contamination of aquatic ecosystems, soil, and drinking water by manure, pesticides, and fertilizers; acid rain from ammonia emissions; greenhouse gas production; and depletion of precious water aquifers. As far as human health, it is clear that the over consumption of animal products has paved the way for rampant heart disease, soaring cholesterol levels, all types of cancers, obesity, diabetes, hypertension, and kidney stones, just to name a few major health concerns. Add to that the use of antibiotics, drugs, and hormones on severely overcrowded, over-stressed animals and you can see why we support vegan ideals. In our restaurant, and in this book, we offer a selection of delicious organic whole foods that just happen to be vegan. Who can argue with that!

Basic Kitchen Equipment

When you're shopping for equipment, there are many items to choose from. Here are some handy basics that we use all the time, and some non-essential but great-to-have items we recommend:

The Essentials

A variety of mixing bowls – Our first choice would be bowls made of stainless steel or glass.

Sharp knives – a good knife is a knife with which you feel comfortable cutting. There are many sizes, shapes and weights. Most home and kitchen stores offer a good selection of professional grade knives. A paring knife, a serrated bread knife, and a 6"-8" chef or santoku knife will see you through nearly any prep work. A heavy cleaver is useful for cutting through hard winter squashes or cracking open young coconuts. We recommend a high-carbon stainless steel blade that is forged, not stamped, and has a full tang (which means the metal that forms the blade extends all the way to the end of the handle).

A good cutting board – a must have! We prefer something with a heavier weight. Lay a damp towel down underneath the board to keep it from slipping around. A wooden cutting board would be our preferred choice, but if you live in a household where the cutting board may be used for meat or poultry as well, a composite material would be best.

Pots and pans – we like stainless steel with an aluminum core. Stainless steel is non-reactive and doesn't change the flavor of the food. Good pots and pans will last you a lifetime and are worth investing in. A good assortment to have: 2 quart and 4 quart saucepots, a 5-6 quart Dutch oven, a smaller fry pan and a larger sauté pan. One non-stick fry pan is useful to have for delicate recipes like crepes.

Measuring spoons – it is very important to get sturdy measuring spoons. Measuring spoons come in sets, with sizes ranging from ⅛ teaspoon to 1 tablespoon. When using dry ingredients, like baking soda and baking powder, be sure to level off with a knife.

Measuring Cups:

There are two types of measuring cups, one for dry ingredients and one for wet ingredients.

Dry measuring cups, which are calibrated for dry ingredients only, typically have straight sides, and come in sets ranging from ⅛ cup to 1 cup. When using, always level off the dry ingredients with a knife for accurate measurements.

Glass or clear plastic measuring cups are transparent and have graduated lines on the sides for measuring liquid ingredients. Using dry cups for liquid ingredients may not provide accurate measurements, adversely affecting a recipe, especially in baking. A 1 cup, 2 cup and 4 cup set would be ideal.

Whisk – this simple tool is used for mixing dressings, making smooth batters and whipping air into mixtures.

Wooden spoon – a good tool for stirring without damaging the pan or reacting with food. Always make sure to wash well after using and let air dry completely before putting away.

Spatulas:
Metal spatula - You should have at least one big, wide, flat metal spatula for turning pancakes and lifting cookies off of the baking sheet without breaking them.

Rubber or silicone spatula - can be used with nonstick cookware and works well for scraping down the sides of the blender or food processor when you're trying to get all of the finished product out of your work bowl.

Offset spatula - These spatulas look slightly bent and can be used for applying frostings to cakes and leveling the tops of creamy batters and cheesecakes.

A blender and food processor are two items that are a little pricier but really worth the investment. If taken care of, they can last a very long time.

Blender (or hand immersion blender) – You can get a wonderful blender for a reasonable price. The more power the blender has the better. Blenders are great for pureeing soups, sauces, smoothies, and dressings. The hand-held immersion blender is ideal for small quantities and for pureeing soups in the pot without having to transfer hot soup to the standing blender.

Food processor – Shredding and slicing blades are very useful for cutting up large quantities of vegetables; the metal 's' blade is used for many tasks, from chopping nuts to blending patés.

Kitchen timer – In cooking, sometimes timing is everything, and it's easy to lose track of time in a busy kitchen. Digital timers that can time three different processes are particularly useful.

Baking sheets – You'll need at least two medium-sized sturdy baking sheets. We use 12"x18" aluminum half-sheet pans from a restaurant supply house, but any non-insulated baking sheet will do.

Baking pans – glass or aluminum, an 8"x8" and a 9"x13" baking dish will cover you through everything from lasagna to brownies.

Cake pans – You'll need two 9" x 2" straight-sided cake pans and a 9"-10" springform pan if you wish to be a baker.

Cooling racks – essential for cooling down baked items. We recommend you have at least two on hand.

Non-essential but nice to have:
Pie plate – a 9" glass or ceramic pie plate is needed for the pies and quiches in this cookbook. A tart pan with a removable bottom is also nice to have, but not necessary.

Salad spinner - if you want to dry salad greens or herbs, a salad spinner is very helpful. You can get by without one, but they work very well. Drying helps keep greens and herbs fresher longer.

Juicer – at the restaurant juice bar, we use a centrifugal juicer, which grinds the food and forces the juice through a strainer. For a couple of recipes, we call for a Champion, or masticating, juicer, which chews up the food and extracts juice by forcing the pulp through rotating gears.

Dehydrator – particularly useful if you are a raw foodist. It's great for making raw food items such as crackers and crusts, as well as for dehydrating fruit and nuts.

Some Notes On Our Techniques

We prepare most of our vegetables with a knife and cutting board. We use stainless steel knives and bowls that will not discolor food or rust. Always keep your knives sharp; sharp knives cut easily where as dull ones tend to slip, possibly cutting fingers and hands.
To avoid over or undercooking, cut foods that you are cooking together into relatively even pieces to ensure they will all cook in the same time.

Blanch – a method of briefly boiling foods. Always add a pinch of salt to the water when blanching to help vegetables retain their color. To blanch, submerge food in plenty of rapidly boiling salted water for 1-2 minutes. To stop the cooking process, submerge the blanched food in ice-cold water for a few seconds. Drian and blot dry.

Chiffonade – To prepare kale, collards, turnip greens, etc., discard any yellow or damaged leaves, wash well with cool water. Stack leaves on top of each other. Roll greens together into a long cigar and cut into ½"-1" strips. For smaller leafy herbs, such as basil, cut crosswise into ⅛" strips.

Slice – cuts are ¼" apart. For a thicker slice, cut ½".

Chop – cut into ½" square or larger.

Dice – cut to create cubes ½". Large dice is ¾", small dice is ¼".

Mince – commonly used for ginger, garlic, and chili. This is done by chopping finely diced foods back and forth with a chef's knife. Push the food back into a pile with the blade of the knife, chop and repeat as needed.

Sauté – To sauté, cook vegetables in a small amount of oil over a medium-high heat, stirring occasionally. Be sure to always heat your oil before food is added to the pan. This helps the vegetables stay firm and prevents the juice from releasing. Also, vegetables retain their shape better when sautéed before adding liquids.

Kitchen Tips

Soak dirty cooking pans and utensils as you go along, to make clean-up easier. Fill your sink with soapy water or load your dishwasher. Pots that were used to cook starchy foods will clean up easier if they are soaked in water before cleaning.

Before starting any recipe, take the time to read the recipe through and get all the ingredients and necessary equipment ready. Don't just dive in, you may regret it later.

Keep measuring cups and spoons handy; you will use them often.

In some recipes, combining ingredients together in a bowl before adding to a food processor ensures a more even mixture.

Pantry

A word about some basics:
Fats
Fat is essential in cooking to impart flavor. When something is too bitter, a little evens the taste; too spicy, it cools and calms the heat. The sense fats add to a meal is one of fullness and richness. Fats are also crucial in building and protecting every cell in our body. Whether it is from nuts and seeds, or fruits like olives, we recommend using only unrefined and minimally processed oils.

Flours
Flour is made by finely grinding and sifting grain. Conventionally, flours are made by using huge steel rollers to break down the grain, causing high heat that destroys valuable vitamins and enzymes. The more nutritious option is stone ground flour, produced by grinding the grain between two slow moving stones. This process crushes the grain without creating excess heat, leaving the enzymes and vitamins intact. Stone ground flours can be purchased in health food stores.

Sea Vegetables
Many have discovered the true potential of these nutrient-rich delicacies from the sea commonly referred to as 'seaweed.' Full of trace minerals, vitamins, protein, and fiber, they are truly worth having in your diet. We use sea vegetables like hijiki, arame, wakame, dulse, agar agar and nori. Sea vegetables are already in most everyone's life - in candy and even toothpaste. If you are new to them, try out a few kinds to find the ones that you like. Most of these are available in Health or Asian food stores.

Sweeteners
Sugar was once a luxury item only the rich could afford, because it was so scarce and expensive. Sugar comes in countless forms. We use a variety of sweeteners to create different flavors and textures. All of the sugars we use are available at natural food stores and are explained in greater detail in this section.

Vinegars
For thousands of years vinegar has been used throughout the world for every thing from a beauty aid to a food preservative. Vinegar has a sweet and sour flavor. It aids in digestion.

Pantry items listed alphabetically:

Agar (Agar-Agar): is made from seaweed. We use agar powder as a gelling agent. It is great for making puddings, frostings, and the traditional health-supportive dessert, kanten. Agar helps to calm inflamed digestion, and to pull together toxins from the intestines and move them out with its mucilage. Agar is tasteless, odorless, and safer to use than its animal counterpart, gelatin. Gelatin is made from ground-up cartilage of pigs and cows and these parts of the animals have the potential for carrying mad cow disease. Agar is available in flakes, sticks, and powder. The powder dissolves much more easily. 1 tablespoon of agar flakes is equal to ½ teaspoon of powder. See Conversion Chart on page 19 to use Ager in place of gelatin,

Agave [ah-GA-vay]: a natural liquid sweetener extracted from the agave plant. The plant's syrup makes a great substitute for honey or rice syrup. Agave does not significantly raise the blood sugar level in the body, making it a great sweetener for diabetics.

All-Purpose Flour: comes in two basic forms, bleached and unbleached, that can be used interchangeably. Flour can be bleached either naturally or chemically, but we prefer unbleached organic all-purpose flour.

Apple Cider Vinegar: is traditionally made from nothing but the juice of freshly pressed apples that has been fermented over a four-to six-week period. It has a strong flavor. Apple cider vinegar can help to maintain the proper acid/alkaline balance in the body.

Arame [AR-ah-may]: is a sea vegetable that looks similar to hijiki. It has long, thin, dark brown green strands. Arame has a multitude of nutritional benefits, including helping with many female issues such as increasing lactation, relieving menstrual pain, and increasing fertility. It also helps to control high blood pressure, and is an excellent source of protein. Tasty and mild, this versatile vegetable is good on salad, or as a warm side dish with sautéed carrots, burdock root and toasted sesame seeds.

Arrowroot: a starchy powder from a tropical tuber that is used for thickening. It is less processed than cornstarch, and can be substituted measure for measure for cornstarch.

Balsamic Vinegar: The best balsamic vinegar is made in Modena, Italy from the unfermented juice of white grapes is both sweet and sour.

Barley Malt: a sweetener that is half as sweet as honey. It is made from sprouted barley and has a nutty caramel flavor.

Blackstrap Molasses: a rich source of minerals and vitamins. As the last possible extraction of cane in the sugar refining process, it's the richest in nutrients of any sugar product.

Brown Rice Flour: imparts a lively, nutty flavor to baked goods. It may be used interchangeably with white flour in any recipe.

Brown Rice: a staple for almost half of the world's population. Brown rice is the entire grain with only the outer husk removed. High in fiber and bran, it has a light tan color,

Pantry items (continued)

a nutty flavor, and chewy texture. It's the rice we prefer at Down to Earth.

Brown Rice Syrup (Rice Malt): is a thick syrup made from cracked brown rice and barley. It has a neutral flavor, and is half as sweet as sugar. Used as a sugar substitute in sweets and desserts.

Bulgur Wheat: a staple food in the Middle East, it is high in nutritional value and has a chewy texture. It makes a great salad or side dish.

Canola Oil: a processed oil that comes from the rapeseed plant. Currently we use canola oil in baking or for dressings in which we want to add fat but not flavor. This oil is slowly being phased out of our cooking and being replaced with other flavorless, high heat oils such as grapeseed or safflower. These oils produce the same result with less processing.

Capers: the pickled or brined flower buds of a spiny Mediterranean shrub, a pungent, tart condiment.

Carob: a chocolate substitute made from the powdered seed pod of the carob tree. Measure for measure, it contains three times as much calcium as milk, and is rich in potassium and vitamins, as well. Unlike chocolate, carob is free of caffeine.

Chickpea Flour: This high-protein flour is made from ground hulled and roasted chickpeas. It looks dry, powdery, and almost chalky; the chickpeas add a sweet, rich flavor. Chickpea flour is gluten free.

Chutney: a sweet, spicy, jamlike condiment served with Indian meals. It's made with fruit, often mango, vinegar, sweetener and spices.

Coconut Milk: has a unique smooth texture and rich flavor. We use an unsweetened coconut milk that has no preservatives.

Coconut Oil: is a wonderful fat. It can be used to produce the same results as butter in baked goods and also is good for high-heat cooking. Many people hesitate to use coconut oil because it is a saturated fat. This is true, but it does not contain cholesterol like other saturated fats. When heated over 240°, coconut oil does not lose its beneficial properties. The body also assimilates coconut oil more easily than other oils, making it less fattening. Another benefit is that coconut butter contains caprylic acid, a fatty acid that helps in the reduction of Candida, a condition of yeast overgrowth in the body. Most coconut butter is semi-refined, taking away most of its flavor, but you can purchase unrefined or raw varieties that have a rich coconut flavor.

Corn Meal: has been widely used in Native American cooking for thousands of years. Corn flour absorbs more water than other flours and yields a drier, more crumbly product. Cornmeal has a sweet flavor and adds a beautiful golden color to your culinary creations.

Couscous: a tiny pellet of pasta made from semolina flour. Common in North African and Middle Eastern dishes.

Pantry items (continued)

Daikon [DI-con]: a large, white Asian radish with a sweet, fresh flavor.

Dates: provide a completely raw and unprocessed sweetener. There are many types of dates. We mostly use medjool dates; they are a larger date that provides a sweet caramel taste. Soak dates overnight to soften them. You can use both the dates and their soaking water to sweeten a variety of foods.

Dulse: This incredible purple sea vegetable is rich in vitamin A, magnesium, potassium, and B–complex vitamins. Dulse's many health benefits include strengthening the blood, adrenals, and kidneys. It is also helpful in treating herpes. Dulse, with its nut-like taste, is one of the few sea vegetables grown in North America and not used in Asia. Lightly toasted dulse makes a tasty snack when mixed with nuts. Available in flake form, it's also good sprinkled on a salad. Try adding dulse to rice and vegetables for a nutritional kick.

Egg Replacer: EnerG is the brand name for a powdered combination of starches and leavening agents that bind cooked and baked foods in place of eggs. It's sold in natural food stores.

Extra Virgin Olive Oil: olive oil is the fat we use most often for cooking. Primarily, we use it to sauté, or for things like hummus, or on raw food plates. Extra virgin olive oil is the strongest in flavor of any type of olive oil as it is the first pressing of the olives. If you are cooking at higher temperatures or making foods for which you do not want to impart a specific flavor, there are better alternatives.

Fermented Black Beans: whole black soybeans that are fermented, then salted with orange peel and ginger. You can substitute red miso, but fermented black beans are worth the trip to the Asian market.

Flax Oil: We use flax oil in recipes that are not cooked. Heat destroys the benefits of this oil. Some of its many benefits include supporting healthy thyroid, adrenal, and hormonal functions. Flax aids in all brain functions and helps maintain healthy nerves, arteries, skin and hair. Flax oil also helps in breaking down bad cholesterol in the body. It is highly perishable; always keep it refrigerated in a dark container, and use within 2 weeks of purchase. Flax oil can be added to smoothies, raw plates, soy yogurt, or salads.

Flax Seeds (Linseeds): tiny oval-shaped beige seeds. Bland in flavor, they are rich in omega-3 fatty acids and very high in fiber.

Florida Crystals: is the brand name for evaporated cane juice crystals. It is available in organic and non-organic varieties.

Evaporated Cane Juice: is cane juice evaporated down to a free-flowing crystal. It is less processed than granulated sugar and retains more nutrients.

Gluten Flour: a high-protein flour made by removing the starch from hard wheat flour. You can use gluten flour to make seitan quickly and easily. It turns a big, messy process into a simple one.

Pantry items (continued)

Goji Berries: an antioxidant-rich, dried, tart red berry from Tibet. They are available at natural food stores and online retailers.

Hemp Seeds: the seeds of the hemp plant. They contain both linoleic and linolenic acid, and a high concentration of complete protein.

Hijiki (Hiziki) [hee-ZHEE-kee]: by far the most popular type of sea vegetable we use. The plump little black strands have a mild flavor. One cup of hijiki contains more calcium than the same amount of milk. High in iron and B vitamins, hijiki supports a healthy thyroid and is good for stabilizing blood sugar. Hijiki is soaked before using and grows approximately 3 times in size, so use a large bowl when reconstituting. We serve hijiki cooked in a simple style with garlic, onions, and ginger. It makes a great side dish or can be wrapped in phyllo dough and baked like strudel.

Hummus: a Middle Eastern dip/spread made of chickpeas mashed with lemon juice, garlic, olive oil and tahini.

Jasmine Rice: an aromatic rice from Thailand comparable to India's Basmati rice.

Kombu: a wide, thick, dark green sea vegetable used in making soups and for cooking beans.

Kuzu (Kudzu) [koo-zoo]: a white, starchy powder made from the root of the kudzu plant. Used for thickening soups, sauces and puddings. Medicinally, it's used to calm headaches and reduce the effects of hangovers.

Maple Syrup: sap from the sugar maple tree that has been boiled until much of the water is evaporated. It is mineral rich and graded according to color and taste; grade A is the lightest, grade C is the darkest. Grade A is commonly used for topping breakfast items, while grade B is often preferred for baking, since its depth of flavor lends richness to the finished product. We use grade B at Down to Earth.

Millet: a tiny, round nutritious golden grain that becomes light and fluffy when cooked. It has a bland flavor and easily absorbs the flavors of herbs and spices. It's popular in India and China.

Mirin: a sweet Japanese cooking wine made from rice, with a distinctive flavor that's sweet but not cloying. It is colorless but full of flavor.

Miso [MEE-so]: a salty fermented paste made from cooked aged soybeans used in Japanese cooking. Available in several varieties, some made with grains as well as soybeans; darker varieties tend to be stronger in flavor and saltier than lighter varieties. We use the lighter varieties in our dishes.

Nama Shoyu: raw, unpasturized soy sauce used in the preparation of raw food recipes. It can be found at health food stores and through online retailers.

Pantry items (continued)

Nori [NO-ree]: paper-thin crispy sheets of pressed sea vegetable. Usually used for Japanese sushi rolled around rice or crumbled as a garnish. You can wrap almost anything in it for a quick, healthy snack. Most nori is pre-toasted, but you can find it raw from specialty stores. Nori contains the highest amount of protein, vitamins C and A of all the sea vegetables. Nori is a good introduction to sea vegetables, and children like it. Try it as a snack for your kitties as well - they go crazy for it.

Nutritional Yeast: an inactive yeast that is used as a dietary supplement and a condiment that has a distinct but pleasant aroma. It is yellow in color and its taste varies from nutty to cheesy. Nutritional yeast is high in protein and B vitamins. It provides vegans with a non-animal source of vitamin B12.

Oats: a versatile grain that can be used in a variety of recipes. Commonly used as a breakfast cereal, oats also work well in baked goods, or as a binder in burgers and loaves. We use rolled oats in our recipes.

Phyllo (Filo) [FEE-low] Dough: tissue thin layers of pastry used in Greek and Middle Eastern dishes such as baklava.

Quinoa [KEEN-wah]: a round, sand-colored grain with a mild, nutty taste and light texture. Easy to digest, quinoa has the highest protein of any grain, is rich in minerals, vitamins, iron, and amino acids, and has more calcium than milk. The 'mother grain' of the Incas is naturally covered with a bitter substance called saponin that should be removed by washing well before cooking.

Rice Malt (see Brown Rice Syrup)

Rice Milk: a dairy-free milk substitute made from rice. You can use it as a replacement for milk in all your recipes. Rice milk comes in a variety of flavors including chocolate and vanilla.

Rice Vinegar: is low in acid and has a rich warm flavor.

Sea Salt: comes from evaporated sea water. Coarse or fine-grained, sea salt has a higher mineral content than any other salt, which is why it imparts a saltier taste than other salts. We used it to make all the recipes in this book.

Seitan [SAY-tan]: is a chewy, meat-like, high-protein food made from boiled or baked wheat gluten. Available as a dry mix, or prepared frozen or chilled in the deli section. The dough is then cooked in a variety of broths and spices. Seitan will keep in the refrigerator for a week, or in the freezer for 3 months.

Sesame Butter (see Tahini)

Shiitake [she-TAH-kee] Mushroom: a rich, woodsy mushroom with an umbrella-shaped brown cap, used in traditional Japanese cuisine.

Pantry items (continued)

Soy milk: a non-dairy milk made from soybeans. Available fortified with added vitamin B12 and calcium.

Spelt Flour: an ancient red wheat from the Mediterranean often used for bread. Spelt has an excellent flavor and is a great alternative for people who are allergic to common wheat.

Spike: an all-purpose seasoning blend of 39 flavorful herbs, vegetables, and exotic spices. We love the flavor Spike adds to many recipes.

Spirulina: a blue-green algae used as a dietary supplement. It provides a protein with all essential amino acids and is available in powder and tablet form.

Sucanat: the brand-name for an unrefined, unbleached alternative to refined white sugar, made by evaporating and granulating sugar cane juice. It retains more vitamins, minerals and trace elements than sugar. It can be used in place of brown sugar, and is roughly equivalent to the brand-name sugar, Rapadura.

Sun-dried Tomatoes: tomatoes that have been sun dried or dehydrated, producing a chewy texture. Sold either dry or packed in oil, they are rich in flavor and work excellently when preparing raw food. We use the dried form in our recipes.

Tahini [tah-HEE-nee] (Sesame Butter): a thick, smooth paste made from ground sesame seeds, a good source of calcium. A staple of Middle Eastern cuisine.

Tamari [tuh-MAH-ree]: a dark, rich fermented naturally-brewed soy sauce. Tamari is made without the wheat used in most commercial shoyu (soy sauce) brands.

Tamarind Paste: a sour pungent-flavored paste made from the tamarind fruit.

Tempeh [TEM-pay]: fermented high-protein cultured soybean cake traditionally used in Indonesia, it has a nutty flavor. Tempeh is less processed than tofu, with high enzymatic activity making for easy digestion. All tempeh should be marinated to remove its bitter taste.

Tofu [TOE-foo]: white curd made from soybean milk. High in protein, tofu comes in silken (soft), firm, and extra-firm varieties, as well as reduced-fat. Silken tofu, wetter and creamier, is best for desserts, sauces or dips. We use extra-firm tofu for most other purposes. Our favorite brand is Fresh Tofu - it rocks. If you see it, buy it. If you don't, and you live on the East Coast, ask your local natural foods store to carry it.

Udon [OO-don]: thick Japanese wheat noodles available in Asian food markets and natural food stores.

Umeboshi [oo-meh-BOH-she] Paste: a condiment made from Japanese sour plums that are salted, sun-dried, aged, and pureed. Contains iron, calcium, minerals, vitamin C and enzymes; believed to aid digestion. It imparts a salty, sour flavor.

Pantry items (continued)

Unbleached White Flour: made from wheat that is refined of its bran and germ. Unbleached white flour yields a lighter product than whole-wheat flour, and is great for making cakes and cookies.

Vegetable Broth Powder: can be used in place of vegetable stock to add a richer, fuller flavor and it's ready in an instant. You can use bouillon cubes in place of the broth powder if it can't be found.

Vital Wheat Gluten (see Gluten Flour)

Wakame [wah-KAH-meh]: a variety of kombu, a flavor-enhancing sea vegetable. Most people are familiar with wakame in miso soup. Some of its amazing nutritional components include calcium and vitamins A and C. It has the incredible ability to bind and remove heavy metals, and to reduce sodium. When cooked with beans, it helps to break down the enzymes in the beans and make them more easily digestible. Toasted and ground, wakame can be used in place of salt.

Wasabi [wah-SAH-bee]: a green Japanese radish with a pungent flavor and a sinus-clearing effect. Wasabi powder mixed with water is used to make the fiery, green paste that accompanies sushi. Available in specialty markets as a paste, powder or the fresh root.

Whole Wheat Flour: is made from hard wheat berries. This flour contains all 40 nutrients of wheat, has a rich full flavor, and creates a denser product than white flour.

Conversion Ideas

To convert a recipe for a whole-foods vegan diet, try the following substitutions:

Beef	Tofu, tempeh, seitan, or beans
Beef broth	Miso paste or tamari
Butter in baking	Coconut oil
Butter in cooking	Earth Balance brand vegan margarine
Buttermilk	½ cup soymilk mixed with 1 teaspoon lemon juice to curdle the milk.
Chicken	Tofu, tempeh, or seitan
Chicken stock	Home-made vegetable stock (page 24) or Pre-made aseptic packaged vegetable broths, powder or bouillon Rapunzel makes a great bouillon.
Cornstarch or Flour for thickening	Arrowroot powder or kudzu root starch Substitute in equal measure for the cornstarch. Mix to a slurry in an equal amount of cold liquid before using.
Cream	Coconut milk or soy creamer
Eggs for binding	Flax seeds. For one egg, mix 1 tablespoon ground flax meal with 3 tablespoons water to make a slurry.
Eggs for moisture	applesauce or silken tofu. For one egg, use ¼ cup of tofu or applesauce and a pinch of baking powder.
Eggs for leavening	EnerG Egg Replacer (see package for amount)
Gelatin	Agar 1 tablespoon flakes or 1 teaspoon powder to 1 cup liquid
Mayonnaise	Vegenaise or Nayonaise These dairy-free alternatives have all the same qualities as mayonnaise, but none of the cholesterol.
Texturized vegetable protein	Crumbled lentils or tempeh You'll get the same effect without all the processing.

Spice Blends

Herb and Spice Blends
Most of these blends can be purchased at your local store or online, but if you have the time freshly preparing your own spice blends are a great way to bring full flavor to any dish. These blends represent some of the most used in our kitchen.
Feel free to experiment with more or less of the herbs and spices you like.

Italian
Dried basil, dried marjoram,
Dried Oregano, dried sage

Mexican or Taco spice
Chili powder, Cumin, Garlic powder
Onion powder, Paprika, Cayenne

Indian
When putting together Indian spice blends it enhances the flavor if you gently roast the whole spices in a pan until they release some aroma. Let the spices cool and grind them in a spice grinder. The smells and flavors from this are a wonderful sensory experience.

Curry powder
Coriander seeds, cumin seeds, mustard seeds, black peppercorns, fenugreek, seeds, curry leaves, ground ginger, ground turmeric

Garam Masala
Black pepper, Cloves, Cinnamon, Brown cardamom, Cumin seeds, Bay leaves, Coriander seeds

Cajuns
Paprika, garlic powder, ground black pepper, crushed red pepper flakes, dried thyme, dried oregano, onion powder, ground white pepper, mustard powder

Herbs of province
Oregano, Lavender flowers
Basil, Rosemary, Thyme, Tarragon

Basics & Sides

These basics may be components of a recipe or great jumping off points for a meal or delicious comfort food side dishes. Try different combinations, use a sauce in an unusual way that you may not have before. Having any one of these basics on hand can inspire a creative cooking experience.

Cooking Beans

Beans are hearty and delicious, and are known throughout the world for their valuable protein. Dried beans need to be washed carefully, as they often have stones. To wash, place beans in a bowl, fill halfway with water and swirl around with your hand to loosen any dirt and insects. Pour off all floating debris or beans and catch the rest in a double mesh strainer. If the water still looks dirty, repeat the process.

Most beans should be soaked before cooking to help minimize gas producing acids. You don't need to soak lentils, black-eyed peas, split peas, or adzuki beans. Place the beans in a bowl covered halfway to the top with water, and let the beans stand at room temperature for about eight hours. (If you need to soak them for more than eight hours, put them in the refrigerator.) When you're done soaking, drain the beans and rinse well.

Contrary to popular belief, salting beans at the start of cooking does not make the beans hard and it improves the flavor. It's actually the acid in the cooking water that will slow cooking. We like to add a 3-inch piece of kombu to the pot at the start of cooking to add flavor and nutrients.

BEANS (1 cup dry)	CUPS WATER	COOK TIME	CUPS YIELD
Adzuki (Aduki)	4	45-55 min.	3
Black Beans	4	1 - 1½ hrs.	2¼
Black-eyed Peas	3	1 hr.	2
Cannellini (White Kidney Beans)	3	45 min.	2½
Fava Beans, skins removed	3	40 -50 min.	1⅔
Garbanzos (Chick Peas)	4	1 - 3 hrs.	2
Great Northern Beans	3½	1½ hrs.	2⅔
Green Split Peas	4	45 min.	2
Yellow Split Peas	4	1 - 1½ hrs.	2
Kidney Beans	2	1 hr.	2¼
Lentils, brown	2¼	45 min. -1 hr.	2¼
Lentils, green	2	30 -45 min.	2
Lentils, red	3	20 -30 min.	2 - 2½
Lima Beans, large	4	45 min. -1 hr.	2
Lima Beans, small	4	50 - 60 min.	3
Mung Beans	2½	1 hr.	2
Navy Beans	3	45 - 60 min.	2⅔
Pink Beans	3	50 - 60 min.	2¾
Pinto Beans	3	1 - 1½ hrs.	2⅔
Soybeans	4	3 - 4 hrs.	3

chart courtesy of vegparadise.com

Cooking Grains

Grains are complex carbohydrate foods filled with fiber and nutrition. They are a staple food around the world, and an essential part of a vegetarian diet. Rich in minerals and vitamins, they are easy to prepare and can be used in a variety of dishes. The combination of rice and beans creates a complete protein. Grains should be rinsed before cooking.

GRAIN (1 cup dry grain)	POT COOKING		PRESSURE COOKING		Yeild
	Cups Water	Time (min.)	Cups Water	Time (min.)	
Amaranth	2	30	-	-	2 ½
Barley, whole	3	60	2 ½	60	3 ½
Barley, pearled	2 ½	40	2	30	3 ½
Buckwheat/toasted kasha	3	30	-	-	2 ½
Cornmeal	4	30	-	-	2 ½
Corn, posole	2 ½	70	2	60	3
Corn, grits	3	20	-	-	3
Job's tears/pearl barley	3	50	-	-	3
Kamut	3	60	2 ½	25	3
Millet	3	30	-	-	3 ½
Quinoa	2	20	1 ½	60	2 ¾
Rice, basmati, brown	1 ½	40	1	20	3
Rice, basmati, white	1 ¾	35	-	-	3
Rice, brown short grain	2	60	1 ¼	50	3
Rice, brown medium grain	1 ½	50	1 ¼	50	3
Rice, brown long grain	1 ½	50	1 ¼	40	3
Rice, sweet	1 ½	30	1 ¼	25	3
Rice, white	1 ½	30	1 ½	20	3
Rye	2 ½	60	-	-	3
Spelt	3	25	2	50	2 ½
Teff	3	60	2 ½	50	3 ½
Wheat, cracked	3	25	-	-	2 ¼
Wheat, bulgar red	2	15	-	-	2 ½
Wheat, bulger white	1 ½	10	2	45	2 ½
Wild rice	1 ½	50	-	-	4

Vegetable Stock

Yield: 1 quart

Making your own vegetable stock is a good way to customize the base flavor of your soups, as well as to use up the odds and ends left in your refrigerator. Good quality organic vegetables make the best stock. When making stock, make sure all your vegetables are thoroughly scrubbed – any dirt will make the stock taste muddy.

Carrots, onions, celery are the most commonly used stock ingredients – they create a sweet and neutral tasting stock. Some vegetables are unsuitable for stocks, such as eggplant, collards, bok choy, and other hearty greens, as cooking them for long periods of time results in a bitter flavor. Use this stock to make soups or to cook with as a low-fat alternative to oil when sautéing.

2 cups each of chopped carrots, celery, and onions,
1 clove garlic, smashed
½ cup chopped parsley (½ bunch)
1 bay leaf
3 sprigs fresh thyme
8 cups water

1. In a medium-large stockpot add carrots, celery, onions, garlic, and herbs, and cover with water.

2. Bring up to a boil, then turn down to a simmer and cook for 25-30 minutes on medium heat. If desired, it can be simmered longer for a stronger flavor.

3. Strain through a fine mesh strainer and use immediately or let cool completely and store for up to a week in the refrigerator or up to two months in the freezer.

Since you can use scraps from cooking, don't be afraid to experiment with new vegetable combinations; the addition of mushrooms make a rich and dark broth, and parsnips add another sweet dimension.

Almond Milk

Yield: 4½ cups

Use this versatile light milk for cereal or in place of rice, soy, or cow's milk in most recipes. Try substituting Brazil nuts or cashews for the almonds for a different flavor and a thicker consistency.

1 cup raw almonds
4 cups water
½ teaspoon sea salt
1 tablespoon non-alcoholic vanilla extract
2 tablespoons raw agave nectar

1. Soak the almonds 6-8 hours or overnight.

2. Rinse and drain the almonds.

3. Place the soaked almonds, water, salt, vanilla, and agave in a blender, and blend on high speed until smooth.

4. Pour the mixture through a fine-mesh strainer into a pitcher, and discard the pulp.

5. Pour the liquid back into blender and blend well.

This recipe is best used fresh, but will keep for 2 days refrigerated.

Baked Tofu

Yield: 8 slices

Baked tofu is a wonderful and versatile recipe. We bake a supply ahead of time and keep it in the refrigerator for a quick club sandwich, or to top a salad for a little extra protein. Top it with a favorite sauce such as teriyaki or peanut and serve with vegetables and a grain for an easy and satisfying meal.

¼ cup Basic Marinade (recipe follows)
1 14-ounce block firm tofu,
   sliced lengthwise into 8 equal slices

Preheat the oven to 350°.

1. Line a baking sheet with parchment paper and brush with a thin layer of the marinade.

2. Place the tofu slices in a single layer on the baking sheet and brush the tops with marinade.

3. Bake for 18-20 minutes until golden, rotating pan halfway through.

Chef's Note:
Most tofu is sold in a plastic tub in the refrigerated section. This is about a pound of tofu, usually 14 ounces to be exact.

Basic Marinade

Yield: approximately 3¼ cups

1 cup canola oil
1 cup extra virgin olive oil
3 tablespoons stone-ground mustard
4 cloves garlic
¾ cup tamari
¼ cup balsamic vinegar
¼ cup fresh lemon juice
1 teaspoon fresh ground black pepper
dash hot sauce

1. Pour all ingredients into blender and blend until completely mixed.

This marinade will keep for 3 weeks in the fridge.

Homemade Seitan

Serves 4-6   (about 4 cups)

Making seitan can be a very messy adventure in the kitchen, but this easy-to-prepare recipe will make you wonder why anyone do it any other way. Using gluten flour cuts down on the time and mess because the bran has already been washed away.

Seitan
1 cup vegetable broth or water
½ cups unbleached white flour
1½ cups gluten flour

Cooking Stock
12 cups water
2 tablespoons vegetable broth powder or
1 bouillon cube
2 tablespoons tamari
1 inch piece ginger root,
  peeled and roughly chopped
8 cloves garlic
1 medium onion, quartered
1 tablespoon Italian seasoning mix

1. Pour the broth or water into a large mixing bowl, then add the flour and gluten flour. Mix just until combined but don't over mix. The dough will be elastic.

2. Divide the dough into two rolls and set aside to rest for 5-10 minutes.

3. Slice the gluten rolls into ½" slices.

4. Combine all the stock ingredients in a large pot and bring to a simmer. Add the gluten slices and bring the stock and gluten to a boil.

5. Reduce the heat and simmer, uncovered, for 40-50 minutes.

6. Remove the gluten slices from the liquid and allow to cool.

You can reserve the stock and store the seitan, in stock to cover, in the refrigerator for up to 1 week, or drained, in the freezer, for 2 months.

Marinated Tempeh

Yield: 1 pound

This basic method will remove any bitter taste from the tempeh. Let the tempeh marinate for as long as you wish – the longer the better.

4 cups water
1 tablespoon extra virgin olive oil
½ cup tamari
4 cloves garlic, pressed
1 teaspoon spicy mustard
2 tablespoons broth powder
3 inch piece fresh ginger, cut into discs
1 pound tempeh, cut in 4-6 pieces

1. Put all ingredients in a 4-6 quart saucepot and simmer, uncovered, for 15-30 minutes, depending on how strongly flavored you wish to have the tempeh.

2. Remove tempeh and let cool before using. Reserve the broth for later use.

Chef's Tip:
Marinate a few packs at a time, freeze and use as needed.

Caramelized Onions/ Caramelized Leeks

Yield: 1 cup

2 teaspoons extra virgin olive oil
4 medium onions or 3 large leeks, white and tender green parts only, sliced thin
½ teaspoon sea salt

1. Heat the oil in a sauté pan over medium-high heat.

2. Add the onions or leeks and the salt and cook, stirring often until they begin to caramelize and turn a golden brown, about 10-15 minutes.

Chef's Tip:
To clean leeks, cut off the tops where the pale green turns dark and begins to fan away. Cut the leek lengthwise from the top, stopping a half inch from the root. Rotate the leek a quarter turn and make another cut, leaving the leek attached at the root end. Plunge the leek ends into a bowl of cold water, swish around, and rub the ends to loosen dirt and grit. Repeat until the leek is clean.

Cashew Rice

Yield: 3½ cup

2½ cups jasmine rice
3 cups water
½ cup dry-roasted cashews
½ cup toasted coconut
½ teaspoon cumin
1½ teaspoons extra virgin olive oil
½ teaspoon sea salt
½ teaspoon cinnamon

1. In a medium pot, bring water and rice to a boil. Cover, reduce heat to a simmer, and cook 15 minutes.

2. Add the remaining ingredients and mix well.

Bread Sticks

Serves 6 Yield: 12 breadsticks

1 teaspoon yeast
1⅓ cups warm water, roughly 104°
1 teaspoon Sucanat
1 teaspoon dried dill
½ teaspoon dried thyme
¼ teaspoon dried basil
2 tablespoons extra virgin olive oil
2¼ teaspoons sea salt
3¾ cups unbleached flour
2 tablespoons extra virgin olive oil, for brushing

1. Combine the yeast, water and Sucanat in a bowl and set aside in a warm place for roughly 10 minutes to let rise. Add salt and herbs.

2. Add olive oil and salt, then slowly add flour until the dough comes together and is soft but no longer sticky.

3. Transfer the dough to a clean, lightly floured surface.

4. Knead the dough for 5-10 minutes until smooth.

5. Place the dough in a lightly oiled bowl, turning the dough over so that the oil coats all sides of the dough.

6. Cover with plastic wrap and let sit in a warm spot until the dough has doubled in volume.

7. Preheat the oven to 375°. Line a baking sheet with parchment paper.

8. Punch down the dough and knead for 2-3 minutes.

9. Divide dough into 12 balls.

10. Roll the balls out into 2" thick sticks and place on a parchment-lined baking sheet. Bake for 8-10 minutes until golden.

These breadsticks can be frozen and reheated. They will keep 2-3 days in an airtight container when baked.

Cornbread

Servings: 8

1 cup whole-grain cornmeal
½ cup whole wheat pastry flour
½ cup unbleached flour
2 teaspoons baking powder
½ teaspoon sea salt
1 cup soymilk
⅓ cup canola oil
⅓ cup maple syrup

The variations on this recipe are endless; you can punch up the flavor by adding any of the following:
1 cup soy cheese
¼ cup minced jalapeño
¼ cup finely chopped tomato
½ scallion, finely chopped

For blueberry corn muffins, mix in ½ cup of blueberries and bake in muffin cups.

Preheat the oven to 350°.
Grease a 9" round cake pan, a pie dish, or a cast iron skillet.

1. In a mixing bowl, combine the cornmeal, flours, and baking powder.

2. In separate bowl, combine the soymilk, oil, maple syrup and sea salt.

3. Add the wet ingredients and mix them into the dry until the batter is smooth.

4. Pour into the prepared pan and bake for 12-15 minutes until cornbread is golden brown.

House Marinara

Yield: 3 cups

⅓ cup extra virgin olive oil
6 cloves garlic, minced
1 medium onion, chopped
24 ounces (or 4 cups) whole tomatoes and their liquid, canned
1 cup chopped fresh basil, or 2 tablespoons dry
1 teaspoon dried oregano
1 teaspoon dried rosemary
1 tablespoon maple syrup
1 teaspoon sea salt
½ teaspoon black pepper

1. In a large pot, heat the oil over medium-high heat, add the onion and garlic and sauté until soft.

2. Add the tomatoes, basil, oregano, rosemary and maple syrup and cook over medium heat for 40 minutes, stirring often.

3. Remove from the heat and season with salt and pepper.

4. Allow to cool a few minutes, then blend the mixture in a blender or food processor until smooth.

Mushroom Gravy

Yield: 3½ cups

1 tablespoon extra virgin olive oil
½ medium onion, diced
2 cloves garlic, minced
1 tablespoon dried thyme
1 tablespoon dried rosemary
1 pound button mushrooms, sliced
1 tablespoon broth powder
  or 1 bouillon cube
¾ cup + 2 tablespoons water
¼ cup tamari
2 tablespoons kuzu
⅓ cup water

1. In a large pot, sauté the onion, garlic, thyme and rosemary in olive oil until the onions are soft.

2. Add the mushrooms and cook until they have released their juices.

3. Mix the broth powder or bouillon cube and water together and add to the pot with the tamari. Bring to a simmer, and cook for 15 minutes.

4. Make a slurry from the kuzu and the remaining water, and add that to the pot. Cook the gravy until thickened.

Will keep for 4-5 days refrigerated.

Peanut Sauce

Yield: 2 cups

1 cup natural peanut butter
3 cloves garlic
¾ cup water
¼ cup + 1 tablespoon tamari
pinch cayenne pepper
1 package Eden Pickled Ginger
    with Shiso, with liquid, leaf removed

1. Place all ingredients in a blender or food processor and blend well.

Will keep for 4-5 days refrigerated.

Nutro Cheese

Yield: 1 pint

Serve with Philly Seitan Sandwich, over nachos or tater skins, or melted atop an Earth Burger for the ultimate Uncheese Burger!

2 tablespoons flavorless oil
¼ cup unbleached flour
pinch turmeric
pinch cayenne pepper
¾ teaspoon dry mustard
¾ cup soymilk
1¼ cups water
¾ cup nutritional yeast
½ tablespoon tamari
salt and pepper, to taste

1. Warm the oil in a small saucepan over medium heat.

2. Whisk in the flour, turmeric, cayenne, and mustard until smooth, then whisk in the soymilk.

3. Add the water and tamari and let cook 5-8 minutes, whisking constantly.

4. Add the nutritional yeast and let cook, whisking, another 5 minutes or until the mixture is thick.

Will keep for 4-5 days refrigerated.

Sprinkle Cheese

Yield: 2 cups

1 cup walnuts, finely ground
1 cup nutritional yeast
½ teaspoon sea salt

1. Process all ingredients in a food processor until well mixed

Will keep 1 month refrigerated, 3 months frozen.

Tofu Cheese

Yield: 4 cups

1 medium onion, diced
7 cloves garlic, peeled and smashed
2 tablespoons extra virgin olive oil
2 14-ounce blocks extra-firm tofu, crumbled
⅓ cup miso
¼ cup umeboshi paste
  or 3 tablespoons brown rice vinegar
1½ teaspoons dried basil
1½ teaspoons dried oregano
1½ teaspoons dried rosemary
1 tablespoon dried parsley

1. In a pan, sauté the onion and garlic in oil over medium low heat until soft, and the garlic can be easily mashed. Transfer to the bowl of a food processor.

2. Add the tofu to the garlic and onion, then mix in the miso, umeboshi or brown rice vinegar, and herbs and blend until smooth.

Will keep for 2-3 days refrigerated.

Tofu Sour Cream

Yield: 2 cups

1 14-ounce block firm tofu
3 tablespoons + 1 teaspoon
   fresh lemon juice
3 tablespoons + 1 teaspoon canola oil
1 teaspoon brown rice vinegar
1 teaspoon sea salt

Tasty Variations:
add 1 tablespoon fresh dill
or 1 tablespoon fresh rosemary
or 1 tablespoon fresh basil
or 1 tablespoon fresh mint
or 1 tablespoon hot sauce
   for a spicy cream

1. Crumble tofu into a food processor.

2. Add the lemon juice, canola oil, salt, and vinegar.

3. Process, scraping down the sides of the container with a rubber spatula until the mixture is smooth.

Using bottled lemon juice will make a more sour 'sour cream'. You will need only 3 tablespoons if using bottled.

This will keep in the refrigerator 2-3 days.

Mashed Potatoes

Serves 4-6

4 large russet potatoes, peeled and cubed
2 tablespoons extra virgin olive oil
2 tablespoons unsweetened soymilk
2 teaspoons sea salt
½ teaspoon black pepper

1. In a large pot, put the potatoes in enough salted cold water to cover and bring to a boil over high heat.

2. Cook until the potatoes are tender, about 15 minutes.

3. Drain and return the potatoes to the pot.

4. Add the oil, soymilk, salt, and pepper to taste. Mash by hand with a potato masher or fork to the consistency you desire.

5. Serve immediately.

You can punch these up a notch by adding 2 tablespoons chopped garlic or ½ cup chopped sautéed greens.

Chef's Tip:
NEVER USE A FOOD PROCESSOR OR HAND BLENDER to mash potatoes! (Unless you want to make spackle.)

Mashed Coconut Yams

Serves 4-6

These yams have a little coconut milk, giving them a tropical flavor. They make a unique, comforting side dish for any meal.

6 cups peeled and diced yams
¼ cup coconut milk
2 teaspoons maple syrup
pinch of nutmeg
sea salt to taste
fresh black pepper to taste

1. In a medium pot, put yams in enough water to cover, and add a pinch of salt.

2. Bring yams to a boil, then turn down to a simmer and cook for about 20 minutes, or until yams are tender but not falling apart.

3. Drain yams in a colander, and let sit for 2 minutes until water is completely drained.

4. With a fork, mash yams with coconut milk, maple syrup, nutmeg, salt, and pepper until well incorporated but not too smooth.

Roasted Yams

Serves 6

5 large yams, peeled and cubed
2 tablespoons extra virgin olive oil
2 teaspoons dried thyme
2 teaspoons sea salt

Preheat the oven to 400°.

1. Oil a baking sheet and set aside.

2. Place the cubed yams into a bowl, add the oil, sprinkle with thyme, and toss to coat.

3. Turn out onto the prepared baking sheet, and roast in oven until softened and browned, about 25 minutes.

4. Remove the yams from the oven and sprinkle with salt to taste.

Cajun Spiced Baked Potato Fries

Serves 4

These spiced potatoes are coated with zesty peppery flavor. Serve them with the Philly Seitan sandwich or just about anything. They are sure to satisfy.

2 pounds washed red potatoes
2 teaspoons Cajun seasoning mix
   (see spice blends page 20)
1 teaspoon Spike
½ teaspoon garlic powder
a pinch of fresh pepper
3 tablespoons extra virgin olive oil
sea salt to taste

Preheat oven to 425°.

1. Cut the potatoes into 6-8 long wedges, depending on size of potato.

2. In a large mixing bowl, combine potatoes, Cajun spices, Spike, garlic powder, pepper, and oil, and toss to coat well.

3. Spread out on a large, parchment-lined cookie sheet.

4. Bake for 40 minutes, turning pan around in oven halfway through cooking time, until fries are crispy on the edges.

5. Remove fries and salt to taste.

Sesame Yams

Serves 4

A sweet, caramelized, sesame treat - always a hit. Serve it as a hot side with any Asian or Caribbean entree.

4 medium yams, peeled and sliced in ¼" rounds
¼ cup extra virgin olive oil
¼ cup maple syrup
¼ cup sesame seeds
1 pinch sea salt

Preheat oven to 400°.

1. In a 6-quart stockpot, bring water to a boil, and add yams.

2. Cook for 5 minutes until yams are slightly tender; drain well.

3. Line 2 large baking sheets with parchment paper, and lightly oil.

4. In a mixing bowl, toss yams with olive oil and transfer to oiled baking sheets.

5. Bake for 20 minutes until yams start to soften.

6. Remove from oven and pour maple syrup over yams.

7. Return to oven for 10 minutes, rotating pans halfway through.

8. Remove from oven when syrup has thickened and caramelized.

9. Meanwhile, toast sesame seeds in a dry frying pan until golden, stirring seeds to toast evenly.

10. Sprinkle seeds over yams and lightly season with sea salt.

11. Remove from parchment and serve.

Sautéed Greens

Serves 4-6

In the age of quick, microwaved frozen vegetables, the simple classic, Sautéed Greens, has fallen by the wayside. Healthful and delicious, dark greens have most of the nutrients your body is clamoring for, and a taste that is savory heaven. Even if you've never had them before, pick up a bunch of greens (kale, chard, collards, mustard greens, beet greens, etc.) from your grocer or local farmer's market and try them out – you'll be glad that you did!

1 tablespoon extra virgin olive oil
3 cloves garlic, chopped
1 bunch kale or other greens, well washed, stemmed and chopped (roughly 4-6 cups)
¼ cup water
1 teaspoons tamari

1. In a large sauté pan over medium-high heat, heat oil and sauté garlic for 2 minutes.

2. Add the chopped kale, water and tamari, and cook down until greens have softened, about 5-7 minutes.

In cooking other varieties, more delicate greens (spinach, beet greens, chard) will cook quickly, whereas the heartier varieties will cook for 20 minutes or more.

Pickled Vegetables

Yield: 3 cups

Pickling vegetables is a tasty but nearly forgotten kitchen art.

2 tablespoons pickling spice
enough water to cover
6 tablespoons apple juice
½ cup rice vinegar
3 cups vegetables:

For Pickled Beets:
 3 large beets jullienned

For Pickled Carrots:
 3 cups matchstick-cut carrots

For Pickled Onions:
 3 cups sliced onions and
    ¾ teaspoon turmeric

For Pickled Red Cabbage:
 3 cups chopped red cabbage

1. Wrap the spices in a cheesecloth secured with kitchen string.

2. Place in large pot with water, juice, vinegar and vegetable of choice and bring to a boil.

3. Remove from heat and let cool. Store vegetables in a jar with a tight lid in cooking liquid to cover and place in refrigerator. Will keep for 2-3 weeks.

Appetizers

As the introduction to a meal, appetizers tease and tantalize the palate with a hint of the dining experience that lies ahead. At the restaurant, we go out of our way to make especially delicious appetizers that are good for sharing. We are always trying to think of creative new ways to make mini versions of our favorites. Many of these can be the main event. Bring them to a potluck or create an elegant cocktail party and pass them around with white glove service.

Try the Collard Rolls – it's hard to eat only two! Our Potato Skins add zip to a casual affair and will delight your guests. Paired with spicy Tofu Hot Wings, they would make a perfect combo for a barbeque party. How about a summertime treat of silver dollar-size Zucchini Pecan Pancakes with Spicy Maple syrup? Oh so tasty! Complete an appetizer feast with our golden Corn Cakes. Fun-sized foods make any meal special.

Collard Rolls Stuffed with Quinoa, Sweet Potato, and Caramelized Onions

Serves 4 as an appetizer, 2 as an entree

This hearty appetizer takes full advantage of winter's bounty. Emerald collard rolls in a golden lentil sauce create a rich feast of color for the eye. Packed with protein, this dish also makes a satisfying entree.

12 large or 24 small collard leaves with stalks removed
sea salt for water

Filling
2 tablespoons extra virgin olive oil
½ large onion, cut in medium dice
1½ cups medium dice sweet potato
1½ tablespoons minced garlic
½ cup quinoa, well washed and drained
1¼ cups stock
½ teaspoon dried basil
½ teaspoon dried oregano

Lentil Sauce
2 teaspoons extra virgin olive oil
½ large red onion, finely minced
1 clove garlic, finely minced
½ cup finely minced celery
2 cups broth
½ cup red lentils, rinsed and sorted
1 tablespoon fresh lemon juice
1½ teaspoons mirin or white wine
1 teaspoon tamari
1 tablespoon dried dill
1 teaspoon dried thyme
salt and pepper to taste
minced parsley for garnish

1. Blanch collard leaves in liberally salted boiling water for about 1 minute, then plunge in ice water. Remove from water & pat dry. Reserve the cooking water.

2. In a 4-6 quart stockpot, heat oil over medium and sauté onions until brown and slightly sticky. Add sweet potato, garlic, and herbs, and sauté until soft (about 10 minutes).

3. Add quinoa and stock and heat until boiling. Reduce heat to simmer, cover, and cook for 20 minutes.

4. Preheat oven to 350°.

5. Lay out leaves rib side down and spoon about 2-3 tablespoons of filling into each one.

6. Fold in both sides of the leaves and roll into bundles.

7. Place the rolls seam down in a baking pan, and pour the reserved collard water into the bottom of the pan.

8. Cover pan with foil and bake for 20 minutes.

9. In the meantime, heat a large saucepan over medium heat. Add oil, onions, celery, and garlic and sauté until softened.

10. Add broth, lentils, lemon juice, wine, tamari, dill, and thyme and bring to a boil.

11. Lower heat to simmer and let cook for 15 minutes or until lentils are soft. Add salt and pepper to taste.

Serve lentil sauce under collard rolls and sprinkle with fresh parsley.

Cornmeal Cakes with Pico de Gallo

Yield: 15 corncakes

When fresh corn and tomatoes are at their peak, make these easy to prepare crispy golden cakes. Top them with our juicy Pico de Gallo and light Tofu Sour Cream. Your guests will think you spent hours over a hot stove.

Pico de Gallo
1 large tomato, diced fine
½ medium red onion, chopped fine
¼ cup finely chopped cilantro, washed well
2 jalapeños, seeded and chopped
1 teaspoon sea salt
½ lemon, juiced

Corncakes
Dry Ingredients
1 tablespoon baking powder
¾ teaspoon baking soda
1½ cups whole-grain cornmeal
1½ cups unbleached flour

Wet Ingredients
2½ cups soymilk
3 tablespoons soy margarine, melted
1 tablespoon egg replacer
1½ tablespoons maple syrup
1 teaspoon sea salt

1½ cups corn kernels
flavorless oil (e.g. canola, grape seed, safflower, etc) for frying

Tofu Sour Cream (page 37)

1. Make the pico de gallo by placing all the ingredients in a bowl and mixing well.

2. In a medium-sized bowl, mix together the baking powder, baking soda, cornmeal, and flour.

3. In a separate bowl, mix together the soymilk, melted margarine, egg replacer, maple syrup, and salt.

4. Add the wet ingredients to the dry and mix to incorporate. Add corn kernels and mix well.

5. Heat a large frying pan over medium heat until hot. Then lightly brush with flavorless oil.

6. Drop 1/4 cup corn cake batter into oil and fry on both sides until golden brown, about 2-3 minutes on each side.

7. Transfer corncakes to plates. Top each corncake with pico de gallo and a dollop of Tofu Sour Cream.

Creamy Chickpea Hummus & Oatmeal Garlic Crackers

Serves 4-6

Everyone loves hummus. Ours is a creamy blend of chickpeas, cumin, garlic, fresh lemon juice, and sea salt. It's easy and nutritious, and people will absolutely flip for these homemade crackers.

Oatmeal Garlic Crackers
3 cups uncooked rolled oats
1½ cups sunflower seeds
¾ cup whole wheat pastry flour
1½ teaspoons garlic powder
1 teaspoon toasted and ground cumin
¾ teaspoon sea salt
½ cup melted coconut oil
½ cup brown rice syrup
6 tablespoons water
3 tablespoons of a mix of sesame, poppy, and caraway seeds for topping

Hummus
¼ cup extra virgin olive oil
2 cloves garlic
pinch cayenne pepper
½ teaspoon sea salt
4 teaspoons fresh lemon juice
2 cups cooked chickpeas
¼ cup water
¼ cup tahini
¾ teaspoon toasted and ground cumin

Serve hummus accompanied by these homemade garlic crackers and/or some raw vegetable crudités.

Chef's Tip:
Using a ruler to guide a pizza cutter makes scoring these crackers a quick and easy job.

Preheat oven to 350°.

1. In a food processor, separately grind oats and sunflower seeds until fine and transfer to a large bowl.

2. Stir together flour, garlic powder, and salt, and mix into oat/seed mixture.

3. In a separate bowl, whisk together coconut oil and rice syrup.

4. Add wet ingredients to dry ingredients, mixing in water as needed. Dough should be stiff, yet pliable.

5. Roll dough between 2 sheets of parchment paper to just slightly thicker than ⅛ inch. Make sure the thickness is uniform throughout.

6. Remove top sheet of parchment and score dough all the way through into 2" squares, then across diagonally to create triangles.

7. Slide parchment onto baking sheet.

8. Mix together equal parts sesame, poppy and caraway seeds and sprinkle liberally over dough. Press in gently.

9. Bake until lightly browned, about 15-20 minutes. Crackers on the outer edges will brown more quickly.

10. Remove from oven and score again. Transfer to a wire rack and cool completely.

11. In a food processor, blend all hummus ingredients until smooth.

Crispy Wonton Packages

Serves 8

Show off your international cooking skills with these bite-sized crispy cocktail appetizers. Shredded cabbage, sweet sesame carrots, shiitake mushrooms, and sliced baked tofu filled packages will go fast but this recipe makes a lot. They may be prepared ahead and reheated before the party.

Wonton Filling

1 tablespoon extra virgin olive oil
2 cloves garlic, minced
½ cup thinly sliced napa cabbage
3 scallions, thinly sliced
5 shiitake mushrooms, thinly sliced
5 fresh snow pea pods, ends trimmed, cleaned, and thinly sliced
¼ cup diced carrots
3 slices Baked Tofu (page 26), cut in ¼ inch cubes
½ teaspoon Sucanat
1 tablespoon tamari
1 teaspoon sesame oil
1 package wonton wrappers
3 cups canola or other flavorless oil for frying

Arrowroot Starch & Water Paste

1 teaspoon arrowroot
2 tablespoons water

Dipping Sauce

½ teaspoon tamari
¼ teaspoon minced fresh ginger
3 tablespoons rice vinegar
3 tablespoons peanut butter
2 tablespoons toasted sesame oil
2 tablespoons agave syrup
½ cup water
1 teaspoon white miso
pinch cayenne pepper

1. Heat a large sauté pan over medium heat. When hot, add olive oil to pan. Add garlic and stir until slightly golden.

2. Add all vegetables and sauté for 1-2 minutes. Add tofu and stir to heat. Remove from heat and set aside to cool. Mix in Sucanat, tamari, and sesame oil.

3. In the center of each wonton wrapper, place a small mound of filling (about 1 teaspoon) and brush arrowroot paste around the edge.

4. Fold each wrapper in half over the filling, and seal wontons by pressing the edge with a fork.

5. Prepare dipping sauce by whisking together all sauce ingredients in a medium bowl, and set aside.

6. In a deep frying pan, heat the 3 cups of oil over high heat.

7. When oil is hot, cook wontons for 2-3 minutes on each side until golden brown. Lay on paper towels to drain.

Serve hot with dipping sauce.

Grilled Zucchini Rollatini with Sun-dried Tomatoes and Olives

Serves 8

People will gobble these tasty and pretty appetizers up at any gathering. The mix of the smoky grilled zucchini, tangy Tofu Cheese, sweet & salty tomatoes, and olives will keep their lips smacking.

2 large zucchini, thinly sliced lengthwise
2 tablespoons balsamic vinegar
¼ cup canola oil
6 tablespoons dijon mustard
2 cloves garlic
2 tablespoons tamari
2 tablespoons fresh lemon juice
fresh ground black pepper to taste
dash hot sauce
¼ cup Tofu Cheese (page 36)
3 tablespoons chopped sun-dried tomatoes
1 tablespoon chopped black olives
fresh herbs for garnish

Preheat grill or broiler with rack arranged 3 inches from heat.

1. Combine vinegar, oil, mustard, garlic, tamari, lemon juice, pepper and hot sauce in blender until well mixed.

2. Brush the mixture on zucchini slices and let marinate 15 to 20 minutes.

3. Grill or broil slices until soft and pliable.

4. Mix the tofu cheese with the sun-dried tomatoes and chopped black olives.

5. Put a dollop of tofu cheese mixture on one end of a zucchini strip and roll up.

6. Repeat with remaining slices of zucchini and sprinkle with herbs to serve.

Stick a sprig of fresh rosemary in each one and sprinkle with minced parsley for a bright, beautiful display.

Marinated Stuffed Mushrooms with Tempeh Sausage and Garlic Aioli

Serves 8

Perfect as a pass-around appetizer at your most elegant affair. This versatile delight is easy to prepare but hard to pass up. The creamy garlic aioli also makes a delicious spread for sandwiches, especially with toasted focaccia.

Mushrooms
24 medium button mushrooms
¼ cup balsamic vinegar
½ cup extra virgin olive oil
¼ cup tamari

Filling
8 ounces Marinated Tempeh (page 28)
¼ cup fresh bread crumbs
2 tablespoons extra virgin olive oil
2 tablespoons tamari
pinch dried marjoram
¼ teaspoon dried thyme
¼ teaspoon paprika
pinch cayenne
¼ teaspoon fennel seeds
pinch black pepper
2 tablespoons unbleached flour

Aioli
¾ cup Vegenaise
1 tablespoon lemon juice
1½ tablespoons extra virgin olive oil
½ tablespoon stone-ground mustard
pinch cayenne
1 clove minced garlic
⅛ teaspoon sea salt

chopped parsley for garnish

1. Clean and de-stem all mushrooms.

2. Mix oil, vinegar, and tamari in a medium bowl. Toss mushrooms to lightly coat. Let sit 10 minutes.

3. Preheat oven to 400°. Arrange mushrooms on baking sheet, hollow side up.

4. Crumble tempeh into bowl. Add breadcrumbs, herbs, oil, tamari, and flour. Mix well.

5. Spread sausage mixture on a baking sheet and bake for 10-15 minutes until slightly crumbly. Remove and let cool.

6. Whisk together the Vegenaise, oil, mustard, lemon juice, garlic, cayenne and salt. Chill in refrigerator until cool.

7. Fill mushrooms with tempeh sausage and place in the preheated oven for 10-15 minutes.

8. Sprinkle the stuffed mushrooms with the parsley. Arrange on serving platter and drizzle with the aioli.

Pan Grilled Mushroom Tapenade

Serves 6-8
This rich and smoky mix of mushrooms, olives, and onions makes a robust topping for crisp baguette with a thin layer of the light parsley-infused cheese. Try any favorite combination of mushrooms you would like or change the olives for different flavors.

Toast Points
12 baguette slices, ⅛ inch thick
2 tablespoons extra virgin olive oil
pinch paprika

Tapenade
¼ medium yellow onion, chopped
1 tablespoon extra virgin olive oil
1 tablespoon water
2 large Portobello mushrooms, sliced
3 medium shiitake mushrooms, sliced
1 teaspoon tamari
1 teaspoon liquid smoke flavoring
¼ cup minced green olives
1 scallion, minced
2 tablespoons minced fresh parsley, for garnish

For the Toast Points:
Preheat oven to 350°

1. In a large bowl, toss the baguette slices in the olive oil and paprika until coated.

2. Spread out on a baking sheet and bake for 6 minutes or until golden.

For the Tapenade:
1. In a skillet over medium heat, cook onion, oil and water for approximately 2 minutes.

2. Add mushrooms and cook for 2 minutes more.

3. Add liquid smoke and tamari.

4. Cook until everything is caramelized.

5. Remove from pan and add chopped olives, scallions and parsley.

Serve the tapenade warm or at room temperature on toast points.

Potato Skins

Serves 6 as an appetizer, 2 as an entree

Crispy baked potato skins filled with creamy Tofu Sour Cream, zesty live salsa and smoky tempeh bits. Top with our tasty Three Bean Chili to make it a delicious meal.

3 large potatoes, rinsed
1 tablespoon extra virgin olive oil
1 teaspoon paprika
pinch sea salt
1 cup Three Bean Chili (page 66)
1 cup Live Salsa (page 112)
½ cup Tofu Sour Cream (page 37)

Preheat oven to 350°

1. Fill a large pot with salted water and bring to a boil.

2. Add 3 large potatoes and cook for 20 minutes or until potatoes can be easily pierced with a knife, but the skin is not splitting.

3. Drain and cover potatoes with cold water for 10 minutes.

4. Remove potatoes from water, cut in half lengthwise and gently scoop out the insides with a spoon, leaving a decent shell.

5. Place on a parchment-lined baking sheet, skin side down.

6. Drizzle halves with olive oil and sprinkle with paprika and sea salt.

7. Bake for 20-25 minutes or until golden.

8. Fill with chili and top with salsa and sour cream.

These can be topped with any filling you like, such as guacamole, black beans, or chutney.

Radiance's Fried Polenta Appetizer

Serves 4-5   Yield: 20 balls

This heirloom recipe has been served for over 30 years in Down to Earth chef Radiance's family, and she is happy to share it with the world.

3½ cups water
¼ tablespoon sea salt
1 cup cornmeal
1 tablespoon fresh chopped parsley or 1 teaspoon dry
1½ teaspoons fresh chopped oregano or ½ teaspoon dry
1 cup House Marinara (page 32)
1½ cups flavorless oil

1. Bring water to boil in a large pot. Add the salt.

2. Turn heat down so the water simmers and add the cornmeal in a steady stream stirring all the while.

3. Continue to cook and stir for 20 minutes after all the cornmeal has been added. The polenta is done once it pulls away from the sides of the pot.

4. Remove from heat and stir in the fresh herbs. Allow to cool for 5 minutes.

5. Scoop polenta into hands with a teaspoon and form into balls.

6. Heat oil in a deep heavy pan until hot, and fry the balls in batches, so that they are not crowded in the pan, until golden brown. Drain on paper towels.

Serve with House Marinara for dipping.

Scallion Pancakes with Plum and Dipping Sauces

Yield: 12 pancakes / 6 pancake sandwiches

Fill these crispy pancakes with smoky soy Bacun and plum sauce for an exotic treat. The fermented black beans come from an Asian food store and are worth the trip.

Plum Sauce
1 cup plum preserves
½ cup fermented black beans
1 cup water
1¾ inches fresh ginger, peeled and minced
2½ small cloves garlic
¼ cup Sucanat
½ teaspoon sea salt

Scallion Pancakes
4 cups unbleached white flour
1 cup sesame oil
½ teaspoon sea salt
¼ cup sesame seeds
¾ cup sliced scallions
2 tablespoons flavorless oil for brushing pancakes

Dipping Sauce
2 tablespoons Sucanat
2 tablespoons tamari
⅛ teaspoon wasabi powder
4 teaspoons toasted sesame oil
½ teaspoon Spike seasoning mix
2 tablespoons water
1½ teaspoons ginger root, minced
1 piece star anise
1 scallion, minced

For the Plum Sauce:
1. Purée all plum sauce ingredients in a blender.

2. Transfer the mixture to a saucepan cook on low heat for approximately 10-15 minutes or until thick and spreadable.

For the Scallion Pancakes:
1. In a mixing bowl, mix together flour, salt, and sesame oil until crumbly.

2. Slowly add water, a little bit at a time, and stir until dough comes together and is pliable but not sticky.

3. Divide dough in 12 balls and roll each ball in sesame seeds and scallions. Flatten into pancakes with a rolling pin, pressing in seeds and scallions.

4. Heat a frying pan over medium heat and brush pancakes with flavorless oil. Fry pancakes for 2-3 minutes on each side until golden brown. Keep finished pancakes warm and covered in a 200° oven until ready to eat.

For the Dipping Sauce:
1. In a blender, blend all dipping sauce ingredients except for the scallion and strain out any solids. Stir in the minced scallions.

To serve, spread the plum sauce between 2 pancakes, making sandwiches, and serve with the dipping sauce.

Tofu Hot Wings

Serves 4-6

No vegan potluck is complete without this spicy take on the finger food classic. The hot sauce was created by our fiery friend Maegan. Be sure to make plenty – these wings will surely fly!

Hot Wing Sauce
¼ medium red onion, roughly chopped
2 cloves garlic chopped
2 tablespoons extra virgin olive oil
1 tablespoon lime juice
2 tablespoons hot sauce
1 tablespoon Dijon mustard
2 tablespoons Vegenaise
2 tablespoons water
¼ cup rice vinegar
½ tablespoon sea salt
pinch black pepper
6 tablespoons extra virgin olive oil
½ teaspoon agave nectar (optional)

Cool Ranch Dressing
½ clove garlic
2 tablespoons roughly chopped white onion
2 ribs chopped celery with leaves
4 ounces tofu, crumbled
1 tablespoon cider vinegar
⅓ cup Vegenaise
1½ teaspoons Spike
1 tablespoon fresh lemon juice
⅛ teaspoon black pepper
pinch cayenne
⅓ cup unsweetened soymilk
¼ cup extra virgin olive oil

Tofu Wings
1 pound extra-firm tofu
⅔ cup flavorless oil

Dredge
⅓ cup unbleached flour
1 teaspoon garlic powder
1 teaspoon paprika
1 teaspoon sea salt
1 teaspoon pepper

For Hot Wing Sauce
1. Sauté onion and garlic in 2 tablespoons olive oil over medium heat until slightly brown at edges.
2. Transfer to a blender and add lime juice, hot sauce, mustard, Vegenaise, water, vinegar, salt and pepper. Mix.
3. With machine running, slowly add 6 tablespoons olive oil.
4. If desired, add 1/2 teaspoon agave nectar. Set aside.

For Cool Ranch Dressing
1. Blend all ingredients but the olive oil in a blender until smooth.
2. With the blender running, slowly blend in the olive oil. Set aside.

For Tofu Hot Wings
1. Slice tofu block in half lengthwise, then slice each half into 7 sticks.
2. Over medium high heat, heat oil in a 9" frying pan.
3. Sift the dredge ingredients into a mixing bowl and toss tofu gently in the mixture to coat.
4. Shake off excess flour and place into hot oil.
5. Cook until tofu puffs and crisps, carefully flipping the tofu over with a spatula halfway through.
6. Remove the tofu from pan and drain on paper towels.
7. Toss tofu in hot sauce to coat.

Serve with small bowls of additional Hot Sauce and Cool Ranch Dressing and some sticks of celery.

Tortilla Torte with Creamy Pumpkin Seed Pesto

Serves 8

This tasty layered torte is filled with sun-dried tomatoes, tofu cheese, olives, sautéed Portobello mushrooms and spinach. The bright green pesto is a zippy addition and is also great to use as a topping for a myriad of things from pasta to our golden home fries or mashed potatoes.

Tortilla Filling
- 10 cloves peeled garlic
- 1 tablespoon extra virgin olive oil for roasting garlic
- 2 large Portobello mushroom caps, sliced into strips
- 1 teaspoon extra virgin olive oil
- ½ pound baby spinach washed
- 2 tablespoons water
- 3 9" whole wheat tortillas
- ½ cup Tofu Cheese (page 36)
- ½ cup chopped sun-dried tomatoes
- ¼ cup sun-dried black olives
- 2 tablespoons nutritional yeast

Pesto Sauce
- ¼ cup toasted pumpkin seeds
- 1 cup chopped de-stemmed parsley
- 1 cup fresh basil, tightly packed
- 2 cloves garlic
- 5 tablespoons extra virgin olive oil
- 1 tablespoon water
- 2 teaspoons miso
- 2 tablespoons nutritional yeast

spring mesclun mix for serving

Serve over mesclun and drizzle with pesto sauce.

Preheat oven to 350°

1. Wrap garlic cloves in foil with 1 teaspoon olive oil and a pinch of salt. Bake in oven for 20 minutes, then remove and allow to cool. When cool, mince.

2. In a sauté pan, cook Portobello strips in 1 teaspoon olive oil over medium heat until soft. Add spinach and 2 tablespoons water, and continue cooking until spinach is wilted. Set aside.

3. Lay one tortilla on an oiled or parchment-lined baking sheet. Spread with one layer of Tofu Cheese and sprinkle with sun-dried tomato, olives, spinach, and Portobello.

4. Lay on a second tortilla and repeat the previous step.

5. Lay last tortilla on top and brush liberally with olive oil. Sprinkle with nutritional yeast and bake for 15 minutes.

6. While the tortilla bakes, prepare the pesto. Toast the pumpkin seeds on a baking sheet in the oven for 8 minutes, until puffed. Remove and set aside to cool.

7. In a blender or food processor, blend parsley, basil, garlic, and olive oil until puréed.

8. Add cooled pumpkin seeds and process until smooth, then add water, miso, and nutritional yeast, adding more water or oil to reach a spreadable consistency.

9. When tortilla is done, remove from oven and slice into 8 wedges.

Zucchini Pecan Mini Pancakes

Serves 4-6   Yield: 12 pancakes

These tasty zucchini-packed cakes are a great way to get the non-vegetable eaters in your life to eat their vegetables. Pecans lend sweetness and add another level of texture to these pancakes. The spicy maple pecan sauce is also delicious on sautéed greens or any vegetables and will keep well when refrigerated.

Spicy Maple Sauce
½ cup extra virgin olive oil
½ small onion, chopped fine
3 cloves garlic, minced
1 cup maple syrup
2 teaspoons sea salt
¼ teaspoon cayenne
½ cup finely chopped toasted pecans

Zucchini Pancakes
1 cup soymilk
1 medium zucchini, ends trimmed, grated
¼ cup canola oil
½ medium onion, diced fine
1 cup unbleached flour
1 teaspoon baking powder
1 teaspoon baking soda
1 teaspoon sea salt
½ cup chopped pecans
¼ cup extra virgin olive oil for frying

For the Spicy Maple Sauce:
1. In a sauté pan over medium heat, heat oil and sauté onions and garlic until soft.

2. Reduce heat to medium low and stir in the maple syrup, salt, and cayenne. Cook for 2 minutes.

3. Transfer mixture to a blender and blend until smooth. Mix in toasted pecans and allow to cool.

For the Zucchini Pancakes:
1. Combine the soymilk, grated zucchini, chopped onion, oil and salt.

2. In a separate bowl, mix together the flour, baking powder, baking soda, and pecans.

3. Add the flour mixture to the soymilk mixture and mix well.

4. Heat 1 tablespoon oil in a large nonstick skillet over medium heat.

5. Pour ¼ cup of the batter into the pan and cook until the top bubbles and the bottom is golden. Flip pancake and cook the other side for about 3-4 minutes.

6. Repeat with the remaining batter, adding more oil if needed.

Soups

Soup is a daily staple at Down to Earth. Even in the summer, we go through it so fast, many can't believe it.

Versatile and satisfying, soup can be enjoyed for lunch or dinner. It can start a meal or be a meal in itself. Prepare these recipes in big batches and freeze them for later, or drop some off to a friend with whom you want to share. All of these soups can be made in advance and re-heated.

Soup is a great food to pull together with whatever you have on hand, especially grain and bean soups. You can also use the season's finest bounty to make something special like Gazpacho or a bright fresh veggie medley. A creamy soup doesn't have to be dairy-based. Using our 100% animal-free recipes, you will see that puréeing or adding potatoes, other root vegetables, or coconut milk can create all the same velvety textures that cream can.

Our recipes are simple and to the point, with many using carrots and onions as a base. A perfect project for beginning cooks, soup is pretty fool-proof when prepared with love and care.

Black Bean Soup

Serves 4-6

This soup is hearty black bean goodness. We use canned beans in this recipe so it doesn't take as long, but feel free to soak and cook the beans yourself, if you prefer. We advise that you cook them before adding them because otherwise the soup would take more water than specified. For an extra kick, add a few dashes of hot sauce and a squeeze of fresh lime. This soup is beautiful served with some finely chopped red onion, tofu sour cream, and a wedge of golden cornbread.

2 tablespoons extra virgin olive oil
1 large onion, cut in medium dice
1 medium carrot, roughly chopped
1 small sweet potato, roughly chopped
2 ribs celery, roughly chopped
8 cloves garlic, roughly chopped
black beans; two 15-ounce cans, rinsed well or 4 cups pre-cooked dried beans
2 tablespoons mild chili powder
1 chipotle pepper, chopped
14 ounces canned diced tomatoes
tamari, to taste
sea salt, to taste
chopped tomato, for garnish

1. In a 4-6 qt. stock pot, heat oil and sauté onions, carrots, sweet potatoes, celery and garlic until softened and browning.

2. Add black beans and chili powder, and cover with water. Bring to a boil and lower to a simmer.

3. Cook, uncovered, for an hour, adding more water if necessary.

4. When the beans are soft, add chipotle and blend; either in batches in a regular blender or with an immersion blender.

5. Season with salt and tamari to taste.

6. Mix in canned tomatoes and top with tofu sour cream and chopped fresh tomatoes.

Coconut Squash Soup

Serves 6

This velvety soup is as decadent as any cream-based soup without the cholesterol, calories, or guilt.

1 medium onion, cut in medium dice
2 ribs celery, chopped
1 medium carrot, peeled and chopped
2 tablespoons extra virgin olive oil
4 cups peeled and chopped butternut squash (1 medium squash)
4½ cups water
1 15-ounce can coconut milk
3 tablespoons maple syrup
salt and pepper to taste

1. Sauté onions, celery, and carrots in olive oil for about 5 minutes or until soft.

2. Add squash and coat with oil.

3. Add water and bring to a simmer making sure to stir the bottom of the pot. Let cook, uncovered, until squash is soft.

4. Stir in coconut milk and maple syrup.

5. Blend in a blender or with an immersion blender until smooth.

6. Season to taste with salt and pepper.

If desired, yams can be substituted for the butternut squash

Curried Red Lentil Soup

Serves 4-6

Spicy, warming, and thick, this Indian inspired soup is flavored with cinnamon, curry, and mustard seeds. Serve it with a big salad and crusty bread.

2 tablespoons extra virgin olive oil
2 medium red onions, cut in medium dice
½ teaspoon minced garlic
2 ribs celery, cut in medium dice
1 medium carrot, cut in medium dice
1 medium sweet potato, cut in small dice
2 teaspoons mustard seed
1 tablespoon curry powder
½ teaspoon cinnamon
1 teaspoon cumin
1 tablespoon powdered ginger
½ teaspoon ground coriander
1 tablespoon minced fresh ginger
1½ teaspoon minced fresh red chili
½ teaspoon turmeric
1½ cups red lentils, washed
8 cups water
¼ cup maple syrup
½ cup tamari
½ teaspoon salt
½ teaspoon pepper
minced parsley and minced cilantro, for garnish

1. In a medium pot, over medium heat sauté onions, garlic, celery, carrots, and sweet potato in the olive oil for 3 minutes.

2. Add the spices and sauté with vegetables.

3. Add the lentils and stir to mix. Add water and let cook, uncovered, for approximately 30 minutes over medium heat, stirring frequently to prevent sticking, until the lentils are soft.

4. Season soup with maple syrup, tamari, salt and pepper. Serve sprinkled with fresh minced parsley and cilantro.

This soup can either be served chunky or puréed and served smooth.

Gazpacho

Serves 6-8

It's never too hot for soup. Take advantage of the jewels of your summer garden, or head out to your local farmers market and gather what the farmers have to offer. You can add any of your favorite vegetables to the mix.

6 medium fresh tomatoes, cored and diced
1 medium red onion, peeled and finely diced
2 cucumbers, peeled, seeded, and diced
1 large red bell pepper, seeded and finely diced
½ cup fresh lemon juice
¼ cup tamari
2 tablespoons hot sauce
½ teaspoon sea salt
1 cup fresh or frozen corn kernels
½ cup finely chopped fresh cilantro
½ cup finely chopped fresh basil, or 1 tablespoon dried
½ cup finely chopped fresh parsley or 1 tablespoon dried

1. Combine the tomatoes, onion, cucumbers, and pepper.

2. Add the lemon juice, tamari, hot sauce, and salt.

3. Put half of the mixture in a blender and blend for 30 seconds on medium speed until finely textured.

4. Combine the blended mixture with the diced mixture and add the fresh or thawed frozen corn.

5. Stir in the cilantro, basil, and parsley.

6. Cover and refrigerate.

For a nice touch, serve topped with fresh avocado slices, scallions or Tofu Sour Cream (page 37).

Mediterranean Lentil Soup

Serves 8

This soup is simple, fast, and delicious.

2 tablespoons extra virgin olive oil
4 medium carrots, cut in medium dice
3 ribs celery, cut in medium dice
1 large red onion, cut in medium dice
4 cloves garlic, minced
2 tablespoons Italian seasoning
2 cups lentils, washed and picked over
8 cups water, + 4 cups water
½ cup tamari
2 cups tomato sauce

1. In a 6-quart pot over medium heat, sauté carrots, celery, onions, garlic and Italian seasonings in oil for 5 minutes.

2. Add rinsed lentils and water and let cook until lentils soften – approximately 20 minutes. Add the additional 4 cups water and cook an additional 15 minutes.

3. Add tamari and tomato sauce and let cook for 10 minutes. Season with salt and pepper to taste.

Potato Leek Soup with Lemon and Dill

Serves 4-6

The lemon and dill we add to this traditional soup give it a lightness and zip that's missing in the country classic.

¼ cup extra virgin olive oil
6 ribs celery, chopped
1 medium white onion, diced small
3 cloves garlic, minced
2 small leeks, thinly sliced
2 medium potatoes,
  peeled and cut in small dice
¼ cup vegetable broth powder or
  2 vegan bouillon cubes, dissolved
  in 6 cups water
3 sprigs fresh dill or 1 teaspoon dried
1 lemon, sliced thin for garnish
salt and pepper, to taste

1. In a 4-6 quart stockpot, sauté celery, onion, garlic, and 1 leek in 2 tablespoons olive oil until softened.

2. Add potatoes and broth and bring to a boil. Lower heat to a simmer and let cook until potatoes are soft, approximately 15 minutes. Season with salt and pepper to taste.

3. In a separate pan, sauté remaining leeks over medium low heat in remaining 2 tablespoons oil until crisp but not burned.

4. Garnish each bowl with some chopped fresh dill, crisped leeks, and a lemon slice.

If you want a thicker consistency, blend half the soup in a blender before finishing.

Three Bean Chili

Serves 4-6

Our version of chili is hearty and satisfying without the meat. Try mixing and matching your favorite beans and different vegetables for a change of pace.

1 large onion, diced
25 cloves garlic, minced
2 tablespoons extra virgin olive oil
4 ounces Marinated Tempeh, crumbled (page 28)
3 tablespoons chili powder
4½ teaspoons ground cumin
1 tablespoon dried oregano
1 tablespoon Spike
16 ounces canned tomatoes or 4 fresh tomatoes, diced
6 cups tomato sauce
1½ cups cooked black beans or 1 15-ounce can, drained & rinsed
1½ cups cooked black-eyed peas or 1 15-ounce can, drained & rinsed
1½ cups cooked pinto beans or 1 15-ounce can, drained & rinsed
½ cup diced green bell pepper or 2 roasted red peppers, diced
½ cup fresh or thawed frozen corn kernels
½ cup tamari
salt and pepper, to taste

1. In a 4-6 quart pot, sauté onion and garlic in olive oil until softened.

2. Add crumbled tempeh and sauté until lightly browned.

3. Add all spices and sauté over medium heat for 3-5 minutes.

4. Add tomatoes and tomato sauce. Stir together and bring to a simmer.

5. Add beans and vegetables and stir well. Cook on low heat, stirring occasionally to prevent sticking, for 20-25 minutes.

6. Add tamari, salt, and pepper and let cook an additional 5 minutes.

Quinoa Vegetable Soup

Serves 6

Quinoa is an ancient grain high in protein. Add all of the season's harvest to create this colorful and flavorful soup. Serve it with a salad and it makes a meal.

2 carrots, peeled and diced
4 ribs celery, diced
1½ medium onions, diced
4 cloves garlic, minced
3 tablespoons extra virgin olive oil
2 small yams, peeled and diced
8 cups hot water
2 tablespoons vegetable broth powder or 1 vegetable bouillon cube
½ cup quinoa
1 summer squash, diced
½ cup spinach, chopped

1. In a 4-6 quart stockpot, sauté carrots, celery, onions, garlic, and yams in olive oil over medium heat for 8-10 minutes.

2. Dissolve the broth powder or bouillon cube in the hot water, pour over the softened vegetables, and bring to a simmer.

3. Rinse the quinoa well and add it to the pot. Let cook until the quinoa starts to plump and soften, about 15 minutes.

4. Add the squash and spinach and cook until the vegetables are softened and wilted.

5. Season with salt and pepper to taste.

Split Pea Soup

Serves 6

When we serve this soup at the restaurant, we have little children bring us their empty bowls asking for more. It is super simple to make and will be a favorite of your whole family at any time of year.

2 small yellow onions, diced
2 small carrots, peeled and diced
2 ribs celery, diced
4 cloves garlic, minced
3 tablespoons extra virgin olive oil
1½ cups split green peas, rinsed and sorted
2 small russet potatoes, peeled and chopped
½ cup tamari
1 teaspoon liquid smoke flavoring
¼ teaspoon sea salt
¼ teaspoon pepper

1. In a medium pot, sauté onions, carrots, celery and garlic, with olive oil for about 5 minutes or until slightly softened.

2. Add split peas and potatoes and stir with other vegetables. Add 6 cups water and let simmer for about 20 minutes, stirring frequently to prevent sticking.

3. Add 2 more cups of water and continue cooking for 15 minutes or until the peas start to soften. Add 2 last cups of water and let the soup finish cooking for about 10 more minutes, stirring constantly, until the peas are completely softened.

4. Season the soup with tamari, liquid smoke, salt and pepper.

Sweet Potato Tomato Chipotle Soup

Serves 6

A great soup for frigid weather, it takes the chill off on a cold winter's day.

2 tablespoons extra virgin olive oil
1 large red onion, diced
3 cloves garlic, chopped
2 ribs celery, sliced
3 carrots, peeled and sliced
3 large sweet potatoes, peeled, quartered and sliced thick
14 ounces diced tomato, canned or fresh
4 cups vegetable stock or water
½ cup maple syrup
2 chipotle peppers
2 teaspoons sea salt

1. In a heavy 6 quart soup pot over medium heat, heat the olive oil. Add the onion and the garlic, and cook for 3-5 minutes.

2. Add the celery and carrots and cook until softened.

3. Add the sweet potatoes, tomatoes, and water or stock and bring to a boil.

4. Lower heat and simmer for 30-40 minutes or until all the vegetables are softened.

5. Add the maple syrup, chipotle peppers, and salt.

6. Purée until completely smooth, either with an immersion blender, or in batches in a blender.

Chef's Tip:
Never fill a blender more than halfway when puréeing hot foods. You'll avoid some painful burns!

Thai Veggie Soup

Serves 6-8

Our customers go crazy for this flavorful soup packed with lots of colorful vegetables.

2 tablespoons untoasted sesame oil
1 small yellow onion, minced
4 cloves garlic, thinly sliced
1 rib celery, diced small
2 medium carrots, peeled,
 halved lengthwise and thinly sliced
12 inches cheesecloth
2 4-inch pieces of lemongrass, smashed
4-inches fresh ginger, peeled and sliced
 into quarter-sized rounds
1 red chile
 or 1 teaspoon red pepper flakes
1 piece star anise
8 cups water
¼ cup vegetable broth powder
 or 2 vegan bouillon cubes
15 ounces coconut milk
¼ cup canned sliced water chestnut
½ cup shiitake or wood ear mushrooms
¼ cup baby corn, cut in pieces
14 fresh snow pea pods,
 stemmed and halved
¼ cup canned bamboo shoots
½ cup broccoli florets
2 tablespoons Florida Crystals
2 tablespoons lime juice
1 tablespoon tamari
salt and pepper, to taste
scallions, sliced thin for garnish
fresh cilantro, chopped, for garnish

1. In a 6-quart pot over medium heat, sauté onions, garlic, celery, and carrots with untoasted sesame oil for 3-5 minutes until slightly softened.

2. Put lemongrass, ginger, chile pepper, and star anise in a piece of washed cheesecloth and tie securely. Place into the pot.

3. Add water, broth, and coconut milk to pot and simmer over medium low heat for 15 minutes

4. Add the water chestnut, mushrooms, baby corn, snow pea pods, bamboo shoots, and broccoli florets, and let cook on low for another 15 minutes. Add Florida Crystals, lime juice and tamari

5. Remove cheesecloth packet, pressing liquid into pot.

6. Add salt and pepper to taste.

Serve sprinkled with scallions and chopped cilantro.

Salads

Many people think that salad is all that vegetarians eat. It's true that salad is a great part of our diet, or of any diet. It's a chance to add fresh, crunchy vegetables to your meal and be creative with dressings and the various ways of preparing those vegetables.

Salad is not just lettuce. Lettuce is wonderful in all of its variety, but there are so many other kinds of salads. At Down To Earth, we always have a deli case full of our fresh salads, ranging from a raw Dark Greens Salad to Baked Tempeh with Maple Mustard Sauce. We offer a sampler that is a delicious selection of salads filling enough for two, or diners can share with the table and add variety to everyone's meal. The Tofu Nuggets are a particularly popular request; people can't get enough of these crisp, salty, cheesy-tasting treats.

Another favorite is the Gado Gado, which we serve as a dinner salad, made of smoky tofu in a sweet and savory dressing, with toasted peanuts and a topping of snow pea sprouts.

Be inventive! The produce aisle is a tempting and inspiring section for salads, but don't limit yourself – venture into grains and beans as well for a world of fun and possibility. Many "side-dishes" from around the world are simply salad ideas, and we encourage you to try the varied flavors and textures of world vegan cuisine.

Maple Miso Dressing

Yield: 2 cups
Sweet and salty, this dressing is highly popular and oh, so simple.

¼ medium red onion, coarsely chopped
1 clove garlic
1 tablespoon miso
¾ cup maple syrup
¼ teaspoon ground ginger
1 cup extra virgin olive oil
¼ cup tamari
½ cup water

1. Blend all ingredients well in a blender until fully incorporated.

Will keep in the refrigerator, tightly covered, for 3 weeks.

Tangy Tahini Dressing

Yield: 1½ cups
Who says calcium is hard to come by for vegans – certainly not if you make this fabulous dressing a staple. Make only what you need because this dressing is meant to be used within two days.

½ cup tahini
1¼ cups water
2 tablespoons tamari
1 clove garlic
2 tablespoons chopped onion
¼ teaspoon dried basil
¼ teaspoon dried oregano
¼ teaspoon dried dill
¼ teaspoon ground cumin
¼ teaspoon black pepper
¾ teaspoon rice syrup
1 tablespoon fresh lemon juice
1½ tablespoons fresh minced parsley

1. Blend all ingredients in a blender until smooth.

Chef's Tip:
Pour leftover dressing over layered vegetables and bake, covered, at 350° for 45 minutes for a delicious, easy casserole.

Fennel Apple Dressing

Yield: 2 cups
This light, refreshing dressing is a delight on any salad.

4 dates, soaked in water for 1 hour
⅓ cup chopped cilantro
1 clove garlic
¼ teaspoon fennel seeds
1½ cups apple juice
1 tablespoon fresh lemon juice
1½ teaspoons grated ginger root
1 scallion, chopped
pinch sea salt
¼ cup extra virgin olive oil

1. Blend all ingredients in a blender or food processor until emulsified.

This will keep for 4 days, refrigerated.

Avocado Ranch Dressing

Yield: 2 cups
This thick, creamy dressing is our raw version of zesty ranch. Avocado gives it body and makes it a perfect dipping sauce for asparagus or steamed artichoke leaves. Romaine is a great lettuce for this dressing as it supports its creamy texture well.

1½ medium Haas avocados
1 teaspoon minced garlic
2 tablespoons minced white onion
¼ cup fresh lemon juice
1½ tablespoons nama shoyu
1 teaspoon umeboshi plum vinegar
¼ cup extra virgin olive oil
6 tablespoons nutritional yeast flakes
3 tablespoons agave syrup
½ cup water
Fresh ground pepper to taste

1. Blend everything in a blender till smooth and store in the refrigerator.

This will keep for 3 days, refrigerated.

Spicy French Dressing

Yield: 1 cup

This dressing has a little kick. With sweet, sour, and spicy flavors this makes a great salad dressing or a dipping sauce for roasted potatoes or steamed vegetables.

¼ cup ketchup
¼ teaspoon hot sauce
¼ cup apple cider vinegar
4 teaspoons agave syrup
2 tablespoons extra virgin olive oil
1 teaspoon brown rice miso
¼ cup minced celery
½ teaspoon minced garlic
2 tablespoons water
3 tablespoons canola oil

1. Process everything in the blender until smooth.

This will keep, refrigerated, for up to 10 days.

Smokey Toasted Sesame Dressing

Yield: 1¾ cups

This dressing is a basic Asian-style dressing with a tiny bit of smoky flavor.

½ cup canola oil
3 tablespoons toasted sesame oil
¼ cup apple cider vinegar
3 tablespoons wheat free tamari
1 tablespoon agave syrup
2 tablespoons toasted sesame seeds

1. Whisk all ingredients together.

This will keep, refrigerated, for up to two weeks.

Fresh Herb Vinaigrette

Yields ¾ cup
This dressing is simple, light and tart – perfect for brightening the flavor of your favorite salad greens. Try substituting any fresh herbs you like, such as dill or sage

½ teaspoon fresh thyme
½ teaspoon fresh oregano
¼ teaspoon fresh rosemary
1 tablespoon fresh basil
¼ cup champagne vinegar
2 teaspoons Dijon mustard
½ teaspoon sea salt
½ cup extra virgin olive oil
fresh ground pepper to taste

1. Finely chop all fresh herbs together.

2. Whisk in vinegar and mustard and salt.

3. Slowly whisk in olive oil and finish with fresh pepper to taste.

This dressing will keep refrigerated for a week.

Croutons

1 loaf Italian bread, cut in ½" cubes
3 tablespoons extra virgin olive oil
½ teaspoon sea salt
½ teaspoon paprika
¼ teaspoon garlic powder
½ teaspoon Italian Sesonings
   (see Spice Blends page 20)

Preheat oven to 350°

1. In a large bowl, toss bread with oil, salt and paprika until each cube is covered.

2. Spread cubes in a single layer on a baking sheet.

3. Bake approximately 6-7 minutes, turning often until crisp.

4. Store in an airtight container; they keep well.

Chickpea Untuna Salad

Serves 4-6

We really don't like to pretend that vegetables are meat or fish, but the dulse flakes in this salad add a delicious sea flavor, and the chickpeas are a good source of protein. So simple to make, you can have it around all the time for a pleasing sandwich filling.

12 cups cooked chickpeas or one 15 ounce can, drained and rinsed
2 tablespoons minced red onion
1 rib celery, finely diced
1 medium carrot, peeled and grated
4 cup Vegenaise
4 teaspoon dulse flakes
1 tablespoon nutritional yeast
4 teaspoon dried oregano
1 teaspoon finely chopped fresh parsley, or 2 teaspoon dried parsley
½ teaspoon chopped scallions
¾ teaspoon tamari
pinch black pepper

1. In a mixing bowl, mash the chickpeas with a fork, then add the remaining ingredients and mix until incorporated.

Serve in a sandwich, a salad, or on toast points.

Chef's Tip:
If you find the red onions are too strong for your liking, rinse them in cold water before using.

Cole Slaw

Serves 6-8   Yield: 6 cups

Everyone should have a good slaw recipe. This basic one can be jazzed up with creative variations such as toasted nuts and seeds or some red bell pepper for a sweet and colorful addition. If you like a kick, spice it up with a shot of hot sauce.

½ head cabbage, finely shredded
½ head cabbage, grated
¼ cup thinly sliced scallion
¼ cup grated carrot
3 ribs finely chopped celery
2 tablespoons finely chopped fresh parsley or ½ teaspoon dry
½ cup Vegenaise
¼ teaspoon minced garlic
1½ teaspoons Florida Crystals
1 teaspoon Spike seasoning
⅛ teaspoon celery seed
salt and pepper, to taste

1. In a mixing bowl, toss all ingredients.

2. Season with salt and pepper to taste.

For added crunch, add 1/2 cup toasted sunflower seeds

Chef's Tip:
The Vegenaise and Spike bring out the savory flavor. The more salt you add, the more water will be brought out of the cabbage. For crispier slaw, add no salt.

Dark Green Salad

Serves 6-8

Add or substitute any of your favorite seasonal vegetables or greens to make this the season's harvest in a bowl. As this salad marinates, it gets better and better.

4 cups dark greens (e.g., kale or collards), washed, chiffonade, and tightly packed
2 medium tomatoes, cut in medium dice
1 clove garlic, finely minced
½ medium summer squash, cut in small cubes
½ cup shredded red cabbage
½ cup shredded green cabbage
½ cup shredded carrot
½ cup extra virgin olive oil
pinch cayenne
½ teaspoon sea salt
2 tablespoons chopped sun-dried tomatoes
¼ cup apple cider vinegar
1 tablespoon agave syrup
½ cup finely chopped broccoli florets
3 tablespoons raw sunflower or pumpkin seeds

1. In a large mixing bowl, combine all ingredients and toss well to coat everything with oil and vinegar.

2. Let sit 15-20 minutes to marinate.

Chef's Tip:
To chiffonade any kind of leafy greens, remove any tough, thick ribs, and stack the leaves atop each other. Roll the leaves up tightly into a cigar shape, and then slice thinly across to end up with strips.

Eggless Tofu Salad

Serves 4-6

The possibilities are endless when it comes to using tofu. This take on a traditional salad is easy to prepare: everything goes into one bowl, and with a few pantry staple spices and a wave of your measuring spoons you can create this addictive salad. Serve on a bed of greens with vegetables and crackers or use as a sandwich filling.

1 pound firm tofu, drained
½ cup Vegenaise
¼ cup finely chopped celery
2 tablespoons chopped fresh parsley or ½ teaspoon dry
2 tablespoons stone-ground mustard
1 teaspoon onion powder
½ teaspoon sea salt
½ teaspoon garlic powder
½ teaspoon black pepper
½ teaspoon paprika
½ teaspoon turmeric
¼ cup nutritional yeast
1 tablespoon tamari
½ cup shredded carrots

1. Mash the tofu in a large bowl, then add all ingredients, blending well.

Gado Gado

(photo page 128)

Serves 4

Our variation on an Indonesian classic is one of our most popular salads at the restaurant. Many people who have tried this would say that Gado Gado means more more or yum yum! A plate of crisp romaine lettuce, garden vegetables, smoky tofu strips, toasted peanuts, and snow pea shoots topped with our addictive Gado dressing satisfies on many levels and makes a delicious meal.

1 14-ounce block firm tofu

Gado Tofu Marinade
1½ teaspoons liquid smoke flavoring
¼ cup extra virgin olive oil
2 tablespoons tamari

Gado Gado Dressing
¾ cup natural peanut butter
¼ cup chopped cilantro
¼ teaspoon red pepper flakes
2¼ teaspoons tamarind pulp
6 tablespoons tamari
¼ cup water
¼ cup canola oil
pinch ground ginger
½ cup brown rice vinegar
¼ cup maple syrup
1 clove garlic
2¼ teaspoons Florida Crystals

Salad
1 head romaine lettuce, torn into bite-sized pieces
6 ounces pre-washed mesclun mix
¼ cup shredded green cabbage
¼ cup shredded red cabbage
¼ cup shredded carrot
2 tablespoons chopped roasted peanuts
½ teaspoon toasted sesame seeds
2 scallions, chopped

Preheat oven to 350°.

Prepare Gado Tofu Mix:
1. Cut tofu into french-fry size sticks.

2. Mix the gado marinade ingredients together.

3. Line a baking sheet with parchment, then brush the parchment with the marinade. Arrange the strips of tofu evenly on the baking sheet and brush the tops with the marinade.

4. Bake for 20 minutes or until puffed up.

Prepare dressing:
Blend all dressing ingredients in a blender until smooth.

Assemble the salad:
1. In a large bowl, toss together the romaine and mesclun.

2. Divide the romaine and mesclun among 4 plates, and evenly distribute the cabbages, carrot and peanuts over the lettuces.

3. Place strips of smoky baked tofu around each plate and drizzle the salad lightly with dressing.

4. Sprinkle with sesame seeds and scallions.

For a more festive garnish, top with a bundle of spring pea shoots.

Greek Salad

Serves 6

One bite of this salad of marinated feta-like tofu cheese, crisp romaine lettuce, sun-dried tomatoes, and Greek olives will take you to the Mediterranean.

1 14-ounce block firm tofu, rinsed and patted dry

Dressing
2 tablespoons red wine vinegar
2 tablespoons fresh lemon juice
3 tablespoons extra virgin olive oil
½ teaspoon dried basil
½ teaspoon dried oregano
1 teaspoon sea salt
2 teaspoons umeboshi paste
½ teaspoon freshly ground black pepper

Salad
1 head romaine lettuce, torn into bite-sized pieces
1 medium cucumber, peeled & seeded
1 ripe tomato
¼ cup Greek olives
½ red onion, chopped

1. Crumble the tofu into a medium-sized mixing bowl.

2. In a separate bowl, mix together the dressing ingredients, whisk well and pour over the crumbled tofu.

3. Cover the bowl with plastic wrap and refrigerate to allow the tofu to marinate (overnight for best flavor).

4. Place romaine in a large salad bowl and set aside.

5. Slice cucumber in half lengthwise, cut into half moons and add to bowl with tofu.

6. Cut tomato in half, slice thin and set aside to garnish salad.

7. Add olives and red onion to bowl and toss with marinated tofu and dressing.

8. Just before serving, add a scoop of the tofu mixture to the top of the romaine and garnish with tomatoes. Serve at once.

Quinoa Salad

Serves 4-6

Quinoa, a complete protein, was an ancient super food used by the Aztecs. Make this power food a staple in your family's pantry.

3 cups water
½ teaspoon sea salt
2 cups quinoa, rinsed well and drained
½ medium red onion, diced
1 large carrot, grated
1 medium red bell pepper, diced
1 cup corn kernels,
   fresh or thawed frozen

For the dressing:
¼ cup fresh lemon juice
2 tablespoons extra virgin olive oil
½ cup finely chopped cilantro
2 cloves garlic, minced
1 teaspoon sea salt
½ teaspoon black pepper

1. In a medium saucepan over high heat, bring 3 cups water and salt to a boil and add the quinoa.

2. When the water returns to a boil, lower to a simmer, cover and cook for 20 minutes, or until all the water is absorbed. Remove from heat and let rest for 10 minutes, covered.

3. Transfer the quinoa to a medium size bowl and set aside.

4. To make the dressing, combine the lemon juice, oil, cilantro, garlic, salt and pepper in a mixing bowl and whisk well.

5. Add the onion, carrots, red pepper, and corn to the quinoa, pour in dressing and mix well.

6. Refrigerate for 30 minutes to allow the quinoa to absorb the flavors.

Chef's Tip:
Quinoa is a wonderfully tasty and nutritious grain, but it comes with a bitter coating called saponin that must be rinsed off before cooking.

Soba Noodles in Peanut Sauce

Serves 4

Savory and simple, these soba noodles are tossed in spicy peanut sauce, served with fresh carrots and scallions. Top with snow pea shoots and sesame seeds for a gourmet touch.

8 ounces soba noodles
½ cup Peanut Sauce (page 34)
¼ cup matchstick-cut carrots
¼ cup thinly sliced scallions
1 tablespoon toasted sesame oil
pinch sea salt
sesame seeds, for garnish
sprouts, for garnish

1. Fill a 6-quart stockpot with water and bring to a boil.

2. Add soba noodles to boiling water and cook for 7 minutes.

3. Drain noodles into a colander and run under cool water until slightly cool to the touch.

4. In a medium bowl, toss the noodles, peanut sauce, carrot, scallion, sesame oil, and a pinch of salt.

Serve family style or divide into individual servings, garnished with sesame seeds and sprouts

Sea Caesar / Cruelty Free Caesar

Serves 4

Light and refreshing, Sea Caesar derives its name from the inclusion of nori and Hijiki Caviar. Cruelty-Free Caesar has the tangy flavor of black olives and sun-dried tomatoes. Whichever you choose makes a fantastic starter or a tasty meal with the addition of baked tofu or tempeh croutons.

Caesar Dressing

¼ cup lemon juice
1 clove garlic
½ tablespoon capers
1 tablespoon mustard
1½ teaspoons nutritional yeast
1¼ teaspoons black pepper
1 teaspoon tamari
½ cup extra virgin olive oil
½ cup canola oil
sea salt, to taste

Salad Base

4 hearts of romaine, washed and chopped or torn into bite-sized pieces
¼ cup carrot, cut in matchsticks
¼ cup shredded cabbage
¼ cup shredded red cabbage

For Sea Caesar

1 sheet nori, toasted and cut into thin strips
1 cup Hijiki Caviar (recipe follows)
¼ cup diced celery
thinly sliced scallion, for garnish

For Cruelty Free Caesar

8 black olives, chopped
8 sun-dried tomatoes, chopped
Croutons, for garnish (page 75)
¼ cup Sprinkle Cheese (page 36)

Prepare the Caesar dressing:
1. Blend all dressing ingredients except oils and salt in blender.

2. With blender running, add oils slowly to emulsify.

3. Add salt to taste.

Prepare the salad base:
Toss romaine with carrots, cabbage and dressing in a large salad bowl.

For Sea Caesar:
Top each serving with ¼ cup Hijiki Caviar, a sprinkle of nori strips, a bit of diced celery and some scallion.

For Cruelty Free Caesar:
Toss with chopped olives and sun-dried tomatoes, and sprinkle each serving with croutons and Sprinkle Cheese.

Hijiki Caviar

Yield: 4 cups

Can be enjoyed warm or cold, and is delicious served on toast points.

1 cup dry hijiki
3 cups warm water, for soaking
2 tablespoons untoasted sesame oil
2 small onions, cut in small dice
4 cloves garlic, minced
1 tablespoon minced fresh ginger
1 scallion, minced
1 tablespoon brown rice vinegar
3 tablespoons mirin
3 tablespoons lemon juice
¼ cup tamari
1 tablespoon toasted sesame oil
1 tablespoon agave syrup
pinch cayenne
salt and pepper, to taste

1. In a large bowl, soak the hijiki in warm water for 15 minutes.

2. Heat oil in large fry pan over low heat. Add onion, garlic, ginger & scallion and sauté for 5-7 minutes.

3. Stir in hijiki and cook for 2 more minutes.

4. Increase heat to medium, add the brown rice vinegar, mirin and lemon juice and cook 2 to 3 minutes.

5. Add tamari, toasted sesame oil, agave syrup and cayenne and stir to coat.

6. Remove from heat and season with salt and pepper.

Spinach Salad with Roasted Balsamic Beets and Spiced Pecans

Serves 6

Beets are at their peak of freshness in the summer, so take full advantage of their sweet flavor. This salad is filled with beautiful gems. It looks gorgeous plated; add some pomegranate seeds for a mine full of rubies. The caramelized nuts are great to keep around as a sweet garnish for any salad.

Baked Beets
4 medium beets, halved
3 tablespoons extra virgin olive oil
sea salt to taste
parchment paper

Balsamic Dressing
¼ cup extra virgin olive oil
2 tablespoons balsamic vinegar
salt and pepper, to taste
1 clove garlic, smashed

Spiced Pecans
½ cup pecans
2 tablespoons maple syrup
1 tablespoon flavorless oil
1 teaspoon tamari
⅛ teaspoon cinnamon
pinch cayenne

---

8 ounces baby spinach, washed

1. Bring a 4-6 quart pot of salted water to a boil, add the beets and boil for 15-20 minutes until slightly soft.

2. Preheat oven to 400°.

3. Drain and rinse beets in cold water and remove their skins under cool water.

4. Chop beets into bite size pieces and toss in medium bowl with oil.

5. Spread chopped beets on a parchment-covered baking sheet. Bake for 20 minutes.

6. Remove beets from oven. Sprinkle lightly with salt. Set aside to cool.

7. Whisk together oil, vinegar, salt & pepper. Add garlic and let sit in dressing until time to dress salad.

8. Toast pecans in a dry sauté pan for 5 minutes. Remove the pecans from the pan and set aside.

9. Combine maple syrup, oil, and tamari in a sauté pan and heat until bubbling. Continue cooking for 3-5 minutes until sticky. Add cinnamon, cayenne and pecans, and toss to coat the pecans.

10. Transfer nuts to parchment paper. When cool, separate and rough chop.

11. In a large mixing bowl, lightly dress the spinach with the Balsamic Dressing.

12. Divide the spinach among the plates, scatter the roasted beets on top and sprinkle the spiced pecans around the edge of the salad.

Tofu Nuggets

Serves 2

These B-12 rich nuggets are crispy and cheesy flavored morsels of baked tofu. People who try these become instant fans, and they are a special hit with kids. Serve these hot or cold as tasty snack or atop a salad.

2 14-ounce blocks firm tofu, drained
½ cup extra virgin olive oil
1 tablespoon tamari
¾ cup nutritional yeast
1 tablespoon dried thyme
1 tablespoon Spike
2 tablespoons oil for coating pan

Preheat oven to 450°.

1. Cut tofu into 1" cubes.

2. Place tofu in a medium bowl and pour oil and tamari over tofu; toss to coat.

3. Sprinkle dry ingredients over tofu and toss to coat.

4. Line a baking sheet with parchment paper, coat with remaining 2 tablespoons oil.

5. Spread tofu cubes out on sheet and bake for 20-25 minutes, turning once during cooking to ensure even browning.

Roasted Tomato, Basil and Corn Salad

Serves 4   Yields 5 cups

3 large tomatoes, diced medium
½ small red onion, diced small
¼ teaspoon red pepper flakes
   or a pinch of cayenne
2 tablespoons extra virgin olive oil
2-3 grinds fresh black pepper
1 teaspoon sea salt
4 ears of fresh corn,
   or 3 cups canned or frozen corn
1 tablespoon fresh basil, chopped
1 clove garlic, minced
1 teaspoon fresh parsley, minced
1 tablespoon Balsamic vinegar
Sea salt to taste

Preheat oven to 425°.
Line a baking sheet with parchment paper.

1. In a bowl combine tomatoes, onions, red pepper flakes, olive oil, pepper and salt. Mix well, and spread out on baking sheet. Roast for 20 minutes turning half way through.

2. While tomatoes are roasting, take the corn off the ears, if using fresh corn, and combine corn with the basil, garlic.

3. Add the corn to the mixture on the hot baking sheet and return to the oven for another 5 minutes. Remove from oven and let everything cool down for about 10 minutes.

4. Add parsley, balsamic vinegar, and salt to taste and serve warm, or refrigerate and serve cold.

Sandwiches and Wraps

Sandwiches and wraps are some of the easiest and most satisfying meals for people on the go. They are also a wonderful way to get a lot of great ingredients into one bite. The zesty flavors of barbeque sauce on our BBQ Tofu Wrap will spice up any picnic. The Philly Seitan sandwich may be new to some but will quickly become a favorite with its deliciously cheesy flavors and delectable sautéed greens. Our rendition of the classic Club Sandwich features the savory flavors of baked tofu, Tempeh Bacun and Veganaise on toasted whole grain toast. The real show stopper is the Earth Burger, a blend of many flavors to create one of the best vegetarian burgers you may ever have.

BBQ Tofu Wrap

Serves 6

Use this spicy sweet barbecue sauce to either grill or bake the tofu for this wrap. Fill it with shredded carrots, romaine lettuce, and diced tomato. Served with corn on the cob, cole slaw and potato salad, this makes a perfect picnic treat.

2 14-ounce blocks extra-firm tofu, drained
1 cup Barbeque Sauce (recipe follows), plus extra reserved for topping
2 tablespoons extra virgin olive oil
6 whole wheat tortillas
1 medium red onion, thinly sliced
2 large tomatoes, thinly sliced
6 romaine lettuce leaves, thinly sliced
pepper, to taste

1. Cut tofu blocks lengthwise into 6 pieces.

2. Put the tofu slices on a baking sheet. Mix the barbecue sauce with the oil and brush half the mixture onto the slices.

3. Flip slices and brush with remaining sauce.

4. Cover and marinate for at least one hour or overnight for extra tender tofu.

5. Preheat grill and grill tofu on each side for 5 minutes or until seared. Or preheat oven to 350°, and bake the tofu on a parchment-lined baking sheet for 7-10 minutes on each side until lightly browned.

6. To assemble the wraps, place a tortilla on your work surface.

7. For each wrap, place 2 slices tofu in the center of the tortilla; top with lettuce, tomato, red onion, and additional bbq sauce; sprinkle with pepper.

8. Fold in the sides of the tortilla and roll firmly from the bottom to the top.

9. Slice each wrap in half on the diagonal and serve.

Add ¼ sliced avocado to each wrap for extra taste and nutrition.

Barbeque Sauce

Yield: 3 cups

This spicy sauce will keep well, tightly covered in the refrigerator, for 2 to 3 weeks, or frozen for up to 2 months.

3 whole dried ancho peppers, seeded and stemmed
1½ teaspoons extra virgin olive oil
2 cups diced onions
7 cloves garlic, chopped
1 cup tomato paste
½ cup vegetarian Worcestershire
⅓ cup brown sugar
¼ cup apple cider vinegar
¼ cup lemon juice
4½ tablespoons mustard
2 teaspoons sea salt

1. Rehydrate chilies in hot water for 10 minutes or until soft.

2. In a frying pan, sauté onions and garlic until soft, and add drained chilies.

3. In a blender or food processor, combine onion/chili mixture with remaining ingredients until smooth.

For a spicier sauce, use chipotles packed in Adobo sauce, and skip the re-hydrating step.

Broccoli Seitan Knishes

Yield: 12 knishes

In this new take on a traditional Jewish classic, we add seitan, broccoli, and onions to make a hearty treat. This is a good way to use up last nights' cold mashed potatoes. Try using other vegetables like spinach and/or mashed yams for the filling. These are a great lunch with a cup of soup or salad and can be frozen.

4 large potatoes,
    peeled and cut into pieces
4 cups water
1 medium onion, finely chopped
8 cloves garlic, finely chopped
8 ounces seitan, drained and thinly sliced
¼ cup extra virgin olive oil
1 cup chopped broccoli
½ teaspoon sea salt
2 tablespoons tamari, divided
1 teaspoon turmeric
1½ teaspoons sea salt
1 teaspoon black pepper
1 teaspoon thyme
1 teaspoon Spike
2½ cups unbleached flour
2 teaspoons baking powder
¼ cup potato cooking water,
    + more as needed

1. Cook potatoes in 4 cups boiling water in a medium pot for 25 minutes or until tender. Drain, reserving cooking water. Set aside.

2. Sauté onion, garlic & seitan in olive oil over medium heat for 5-10 minutes. Add broccoli and cook 2 minutes more.

3. Mash the potatoes.

4. Stir half of the mashed potatoes into the broccoli/seitan mixture. Season with ½ teaspoon salt and 1 tablespoon tamari. Set aside.

5. Preheat oven to 375°. Line a baking sheet with parchment paper.

6. Mix the remaining potatoes with the turmeric, 1½ teaspoon salt, pepper, thyme, Spike, flour and baking powder to create dough. Add ¼ cup of the potato water and knead. Add more water as need until dough is soft and comes together.

7. Turn out onto floured surface and knead for a few minutes. Roll out into a ¼" thick rectangle and cut into 12 4"x4" squares.

8. Scoop ½ cup of filling onto the middle of each of the squares. Bringing opposite corners together, fold the dough over the filling and pinch closed to form a pouch.

9. Place pouches seam side down on lined baking sheet. Brush tops with oil and bake 20-25 minutes, until golden brown.

Chef's Tip:
Dough squares may be rolled out more as needed to accommodate filling.

Club Sandwich

Serves 1

This mouthwatering version of a country club favorite will get you into any club you desire. Smokey tempeh and baked tofu pair up to make it one of our all time favorites.

3 slices whole wheat bread
Vegenaise to taste
2 slices Baked Tofu (page 26)
3 slices Tempeh Bacun (page 172)
2 slices tomato
2 leaves lettuce

1. Lightly toast 3 slices of bread.

2. Spread each slice with Vegenaise to taste.

3. On the bottom slice, lay 1 to 2 pieces of tofu & on top of that, 3 tempeh strips.

4. Cover with middle slice of bread, and layer on tomato, then the lettuce.

5. Cover with last slice of bread and slice diagonally into 2 or 4 pieces, using toothpicks to keep layers together.

Earth Burger

Yield: 12 burgers

Pantry staples come together to create the best burger on this planet. A blend of tofu, brown rice, oats, sunflower seeds, vegetables and spices, this is a crowd pleaser. Even though it makes a big batch, it won't make it to the freezer.

1 14-ounce block firm tofu, pressed
1 tablespoon extra virgin olive oil
1 tablespoon canola oil
1 medium onion, chopped fine
2 cloves garlic, chopped fine
1 cup finely chopped carrot
1 cup quick cooking oats
1½ cups sunflower seeds
2 cups cooked brown rice
1 tablespoon fresh parsley, chopped
1 tablespoon Spike
1 tablespoon white miso
1 tablespoon lemon juice
1 tablespoon dried thyme
1 tablespoon dried basil
3 tablespoons tamari
¾ cup bread crumbs
6 tablespoons water
oil, for brushing

Preheat oven to 350°.

1. In a large bowl, mash tofu thoroughly and set aside.

2. In a medium pan, sauté onion, garlic and carrots in canola and olive oil over medium heat until soft but not brown. Transfer to the bowl with the mashed tofu.

3. Add the remaining ingredients except the water and oil for brushing to the tofu mixture.

4. Process in batches in a food processor until everything is well blended, adding the water a tablespoon at a time until the mixture binds together.

5. Form into 1 cup burgers.

6. Place the burgers on a parchment-lined baking sheet brushed with oil and bake in the oven for 20 minutes, turning baking sheet halfway through cooking to ensure even browning.

After cooking, these burgers can be frozen in an airtight container for up to 2 months. Thaw fully before reheating.

Chef's Tip:
To press tofu, place a block of tofu between two plates. Place a heavy object (like a can or two of beans) on top of the top plate and let sit for a half hour. Pour off the water, and pat the tofu dry.

Philly Seitan Sandwich

Yield: 4 sandwiches

East Coast flavor in a bun. We have transformed this Philly-style sandwich into a vegan version made even more scrumptious with thinly sliced seitan and caramelized onions, to which we've added calcium rich sautéed greens, and b vitamin rich nutritional yeast cheese. Serve these with oven-baked sweet potato fries for all out decadence.

2 12-inch loaves Italian bread
4 cups thinly sliced seitan
¼ cup tamari
3 tablespoons extra virgin olive oil
½ cup Caramelized Onions (page 29)
Nutro Cheese (page 35)
Sautéed Greens (page 42)
roasted red peppers, sliced thin

Preheat oven to 350°.

1. Toss the sliced seitan with tamari and olive oil. Spread out on a parchment-lined baking sheet and bake for 6-8 minutes or until golden.

2. Slice loaves in half lengthwise and place in oven a minute or two to warm.

3. Mix the seitan and the caramelized onions together and spread out on the split loaves.

4. Smother with the Nutro Cheese and serve with sautéed greens and roasted red peppers.

5. Fold the bread over the filling and cut each loaf in half to create 4 sandwiches.

Falafel

Serves 2   Yield: 12 falafel

All the traditional flavors of the Middle East, wrapped in freshly made flat bread. Serve accompanied with Tahini Sauce and herbed Cucumber Salad

½ cup bulgur
½ teaspoon extra virgin olive oil
1 cup cooked chickpeas or
　one 15 ounce can, drained and rinsed
½ large onion, cut in small dice
1 tablespoon chopped fresh parsley
　or 1 teaspoon dry
1 tablespoon flax seeds
2 cloves garlic
½ teaspoon salt
1 teaspoon red pepper flakes
1 teaspoon cumin
⅛ teaspoon ground coriander
extra virgin olive oil, for baking
Tahini Sauce (recipe follows)
2 whole-wheat pita breads, halved

shredded lettuce, for serving
sliced tomato, for serving

Preheat oven to 350°.

1. Soak bulgur in warm water to cover for at least ½ hour.

2. Sauté half the onion in 1 teaspoon olive oil until slightly soft.

3. Combine chickpeas, the onion, parsley, flax seeds, garlic, salt, and spices in a food processor and blend until combined but not totally smooth.

4. Drain bulgur and add enough to the chickpea mixture so that the mixture is no longer sticky.

5. Coat a large baking sheet with olive oil.

6. Form falafel mixture into golf ball-sized balls and flatten slightly. Place, well spaced, on the oiled baking sheet.

7. Bake for about 15 minutes or until golden brown, turning sheet around halfway through baking time.

8. Serve in a warm pita with shredded lettuce, diced tomato and tahini sauce.

Tahini Sauce

Yield: ¾ cup

¼ cup tahini
6 tablespoons water
1 teaspoon fresh lemon juice
2 cloves garlic, minced
Pinch sea salt

1. Combine all sauce ingredients in a blender, and blend until smooth.

Cucumber Salad

Serves 4

2 cups plain vegan soy yogurt
4 tablespoons minced fresh mint leaves
2 tablespoons lemon juice
2 small cloves garlic, minced
2 pinches white pepper
2 medium cucumbers peeled, seeded and chopped
sea salt to taste

1. Mix all ingredients and chill.

Gyros

Serves 4

This sandwich takes some time to prepare but you'll find it is well worth the effort when you wrap your mouth around these juicy layers of seitan with zesty Moroccan-style marinade in homemade bread or whole-wheat pita filled with crisp romaine and tomatoes dressed with a creamy cool cucumber sauce.

Gyro Bread (recipe follows) or
4 whole-wheat pita breads

Cucumber Dressing
1 12.3 ounce package firm Silken Lite Tofu, drained and crumbled
½ cup peeled and finely chopped cucumber
1 tablespoon extra virgin olive oil
2 teaspoons fresh lemon juice
¼ teaspoon sea salt
¼ teaspoon black pepper

Moroccan Marinade
1 cup tomato juice
⅓ cup fresh orange juice
⅓ cup fresh lemon juice
2 tablespoons tamari
3 cloves garlic
2 tablespoons rice syrup
⅓ teaspoon red pepper flakes
⅔ teaspoon ground coriander
⅓ teaspoon cinnamon
1⅓ teaspoons cumin
⅔ teaspoon fennel seeds, ground
1⅓ teaspoons fresh minced ginger
1½ teaspoons balsamic vinegar
canola oil, for frying
2 cups seitan, thinly sliced
2 cups bite-sized pieces romaine lettuce leaves
1 tomato, chopped
1 small red onion, sliced thin

1. To make the dressing, put the tofu, cucumber, olive oil, lemon juice, salt and pepper in a blender or food processor and process to a chunky sauce. Set aside.

2. In a small bowl, combine the marinade ingredients and whisk together.

3. Coat a skillet with a thin layer of canola oil over medium heat.

4. When hot, lay seitan slices in a single layer and brown on both sides.

5. Pour marinade into skillet over browned tofu and cook for 3-5 minutes.

6. Remove from heat and set aside.

7. To assemble the sandwiches, place Gyro Bread or pitas on a clean surface and divide seitan equally among them.

8. Top the seitan with lettuce, tomato and onion, then top with dressing.

9. Fold bread over and eat taco style.

Gyro Bread

Yield: 4-6 loaves

2¼ cups warm water, approximately 104°
1 tablespoon dry yeast
1 tablespoon Sucanat
5 tablespoons extra virgin olive oil, divided
1½ teaspoons sea salt
3 cups unbleached pastry flour

Preheat oven to 400°.

1. In a medium sized bowl, combine the water, yeast and Sucanat. Let sit in warm spot for 5 minutes until foamy.

2. Mix in the olive oil and salt.

3. Add flour slowly until the dough comes together - it should be soft, but not too sticky.

4. Turn out onto a lightly floured work surface and knead dough for 10 minutes, until it is smooth and elastic.

5. Coat the inside of a clean bowl with 2 tablespoons of olive oil and place dough inside; roll dough around in the oiled bowl to coat all surfaces.

6. Cover the dough with plastic wrap and let rise for at about 20-30 minutes, until doubled in size.

7. Lightly knead the dough and divide into four to six balls.

8. Roll out each piece to a thin rectangle approximately 5 X 7 inches. Poke all over with a fork, place on a baking sheet and bake for 3-5 minutes.

9. Wrap the hot bread in foil to keep it pliable until serving.

10. The breads can be reheated by putting in a 200° oven for 3-4 minutes.

If you don't have the time to make the bread, you can easily substitute pita for the gyro bread.

Quinoa Avocado Wrap with Orange Baked Tofu

Yield: 6 wraps

The combination of quinoa, tofu and avocado provides your body with all the essential fats and protein needed to keep it healthy and satisfied. Fill these with any of your favorite vegetables to create a nutritious, flavorful and satisfying lunch.

Tofu Marinade
- 1 cup orange juice
- ½ cup lemon juice
- ¼ cup brown rice syrup or maple syrup
- ½ cup chopped cilantro
- 1 teaspoon extra virgin olive oil
- ½ teaspoon sea salt
- 1 14-ounce block extra-firm tofu, cut in ¼" slices

- 2 cups cooked quinoa
- 3 ripe avocadoes, peeled, pitted and sliced
- 2 large tomatoes, sliced thin
- 1 medium onion, sliced thin
- 1 medium cucumber, peeled, seeded and sliced thin
- 6 large whole wheat tortillas

Prepare the Tofu:

1. Make the marinade by putting the orange juice, lemon juice, rice syrup, cilantro, cumin, salt and olive oil in a blender and mixing until well combined.

2. Place the tofu slabs in a single layer in a shallow baking dish and pour mixture over top. Cover and let marinade for 30-60 minutes.

3. Preheat oven to 375° and bake tofu on a parchment-lined baking sheet for 18 minutes.

Assemble the wraps

1. Place a tortilla on your work surface.

2. For each tortilla, put ⅓ cup of quinoa in the center and top with ½ sliced avocado, tomato, onion, and cucumber. Cut one slab of tofu per wrap into strips and scatter on top.

3. Fold both sides of the tortilla in and roll tightly from bottom to top.

4. Slice each wrap in half on the diagonal and serve.

Tofu Parmesan Sandwich

Serves 6

These flavor filled patties are made by blending tofu with Italian spices, coating with breadcrumbs and baking. Serve these patties as a sandwich with sautéed greens or over pasta with marinara for a delightful meal.

1 medium yellow onion, diced
4 cloves garlic
2 tablespoons extra virgin olive oil
2 tablespoons Italian seasoning
2 14-ounce blocks firm tofu, drained
1 teaspoon minced fresh parsley
1 teaspoon sea salt
½ teaspoon pepper
2 tablespoons nutritional yeast
1 tablespoon garlic powder
3 tablespoons vegetable broth powder
  or 1 vegan bouillon cube,
  dissolved in 2 tablespoons hot water
¼ cup dry white wine, mirin or water
1 tablespoon tamari
2 cups bread crumbs, divided

6 rolls of your choice
1 cup vegan mozzarella, shredded
Sprinkle Cheese (page 36), for sprinkling

Preheat oven to 375°.
Lightly oil a baking sheet and set aside.

1. Sauté onions and garlic in olive oil over medium heat until golden, then stir in the Italian seasoning.

2. Crumble tofu into a medium mixing bowl, and add parsley, salt, pepper, nutritional yeast and garlic powder. Mix to incorporate everything. Add the sautéed onion and garlic to the tofu mix.

3. Add the broth/wine/tamari mixture to the sauté pan. Increase heat to medium and whisk the liquid to deglaze the pan. Add to the tofu mix.

4. Transfer the tofu mixture to the bowl of a food processor and process, adding 1 cup of bread crumbs until mixture comes together and is a bit sticky.

5. Pour the remaining cup of bread crumbs into a shallow pan. Portion the tofu mixture out into golf ball sized balls, flatten into patties and coat each side with the bread crumbs. Place on the oiled baking sheet and bake for 12 minutes or until golden.

6. Place 1 patty on a split roll, sprinkle with vegan mozzarella and bake until cheese is bubbly. Top with some Sprinkle Cheese, fold sandwich closed and enjoy.

Wheatball Sub (a.k.a Wheatball Hoagie, Wheatball Grinder, Wheatball Hero)

Serves 4

This is a classic Italian meatball sub transformed with wheat, the classic American grain, into a healthful vegan lunchtime sandwich. For the pasta lover, these wheatballs can also be substituted in the traditional spaghetti and meatballs.

1½ pounds seitan, about 5 cups
2 cups fresh bread crumbs, tightly packed
¼ cup extra virgin olive oil
2 medium onions, diced
6 cloves garlic, minced
1½ cups dry bread crumbs
1 cup tomato sauce
1 tablespoon Spike
1 tablespoon Italian seasoning
1 tablespoon + 1 teaspoon tamari
2 tablespoons dried basil
4½ teaspoons dried oregano
4½ teaspoons dried rosemary
extra virgin olive oil, for brushing
2 submarine rolls
1½ cups House Marinara (page 32), for spooning over rolls
Sautéed Greens (page 42)
Sprinkle Cheese (page 36), for sprinkling

Preheat oven to 350°.

1. In a food processor fitted with the metal blade, grind the seitan until crumbled fine.

2. Add the fresh bread crumbs to the processing bowl with the seitan.

3. In a large pan, warm the olive oil over medium heat and add the onion and garlic. Sauté until soft, then add to the processing bowl with the seitan.

4. Add all the remaining ingredients, and process together in the food processor until a dough-like mixture comes together.

5. Scoop out ¼ cup measures of the mixture and roll into balls.

6. Place the wheatballs on a parchment-lined baking sheet and lightly oil the tops of the wheatballs.

7. Bake for 15 minutes.

8. To assemble sandwiches, place wheatballs in a split sub roll and top with House Marinara, sautéed greens and sprinkle cheese.

Live Foods

Enzymes help us digest and assimilate everything we eat, giving us energy and health benefits. Proponents of raw foods believe that as we eat cooked food, the body has to increase its digestive capacity. By adding raw foods such as salads we aid in the digestive process and give our body a much-needed break, saving those valuable enzymes for that extra big piece of Chocolate Ganache cake we occasionally splurge on!

Nuts and seeds pack raw foods with protein and good fats, too. Avocado, a rich source of healthy vegan fat, can be a key ingredient in countless sauces, raw soups, salads, dips or even a raw fruit smoothie. We use dehydrators for some of these recipes, such as the Pizza Crackers, but try any of the cheeses or sauces with cabbage leaves or crisp romaine.

A perfect example of using live vegetables instead of cooked is the Leaf Wrap filled with guacamole and zesty sun-dried tomato pâté. If you are really craving crackers and don't have a dehydrator, some natural markets carry "raw" crackers and pre-made treats, and you can also order them on-line.

These recipe ideas are so packed with enzymes and taste, your oven might stay off for a while after you try them.

Adam's Pink Lady Apple Salsa

Serves 6

"Pink Lady apples are my favorite because of their balanced flavor. They are usually quite tart, a bit sweet, crisp, and beautifully colored. This salsa is delicious on spinach salads or as a refreshing compliment to a grilled tofu or seitan dish."
– Adam

3 medium Pink Lady apples
¼ cup minced fresh cilantro
¼ cup minced fresh mint
½ cup thinly sliced scallions
1 medium jalapeño, seeded and minced
2 limes, zested and juiced
pinch sea salt, to taste

1. Core and finely dice the apples.

2. Toss with the remaining ingredients and refrigerate for at least one hour in a covered container.

3. Toss again prior to use to coat with juices and marry flavors.

Curried Almond Pâté

Serves 4   Yield: 1 cup

Almonds are the perfect, easily digestible nut for humans, especially after soaking. This pâté will fill you up and is chock full of protein, calcium and great flavor. Serve it in Napa cabbage leaves with the Fennel Apple Dressing (page 73).

½ cup raw almonds, soaked overnight
1 clove garlic
1½ teaspoons chopped scallion
¼ cup extra virgin olive oil
½ teaspoon curry powder
1 teaspoon nama shoyu
2 tablespoons water
1½ teaspoons chopped fresh cilantro
¾ teaspoon light agave syrup

1. In a food processor, blend garlic, scallions, curry powder and water until evenly incorporated.

2. With the motor running, slowly add soaked almonds through the chute. Stop machine halfway through to scrape down sides.

3. Add olive oil and nama shoyu, and pulse until incorporated.

4. Add cilantro and agave, and blend until smooth.

5. Transfer the mixture into a covered container and refrigerate for a couple of hours to allow the flavors to marry.

Flax Crackers

Yield: 12 2" square crackers

Sesame seeds bring calcium to this savory, crisp dehydrated cracker, and fiber and omegas come from the flax seeds. Try using the same base recipe and experiment with a variety of seasonings.

1 cup raw sesame seeds
1 cup flax seeds
2 cups water
1½ teaspoons garlic powder
1½ teaspoons sea salt
1½ teaspoons minced fresh ginger
2 tablespoons minced scallion
¼ cup nutritional yeast

1. Combine ingredients and soak for at least 15 minutes, until the mixture thickens and becomes gel-like.

2. Halve mixture and spread thinly onto 2 Teflex dehydrator sheets.

3. Score the dough into 12 crackers and dehydrate at 115° for at least 12 hours. Crackers should be crisp when done

Leaf Wraps

(photo page 125)

Serves 6-8

This combination of Brazil nut and sun dried tomatoes layered with guacamole, fresh tomatoes and shredded spinach is as delectable as it is colorful. We use the nutritional and versatile sprinkle cheese on top to add a zest that makes these reminiscent of tacos.

1 head romaine lettuce
Sun-Dried Tomato Pâté (recipe follows)
Sprinkle Cheese (page 36)

1. Wash the lettuce and separate into leaves.

2. Spoon 2 tablespoons Sun-Dried Tomato Pâté into the center of each leaf.

3. Serve 4 to a plate and sprinkle liberally with Sprinkle Cheese.

Sun-Dried Tomato Pâté

Yield: 1 pint

¾ cup sun-dried tomatoes
6 tablespoons raw sunflower seeds
½ cup Brazil nuts
1½ cloves garlic
1 tablespoon chopped fresh parsley
2 tablespoons chopped scallions
2 tablespoons extra virgin olive oil
¼ large lemon, juiced and zested
¼ teaspoon fresh ground black pepper
pinch cayenne pepper
2 tablespoons chopped black olives

1. Soak the sun-dried tomatoes in 1 cup of warm water until soft, about 1 hour. Drain, reserving the soaking liquid.

2. In a food processor, blend the sunflower seeds and Brazil nuts until fine. Transfer to a bowl and set aside.

3. Combine ¾ cup of the reserved soaking water, the sun-dried tomatoes and the rest of the ingredients except for 1 tablespoon of black olives in the food processor, and process until smooth.

4. Add the processed nuts and blend until smooth. Stir in the remaining 1 tablespoon of black olives.

This zesty pâté keeps for 4-5 days refrigerated.

Live Lasagna

Serves 6

A show stopping live entrée. This creamy light lasagna uses cashews to create a cheese-like spread layered with fresh yellow squash, zucchini and sweet sun dried tomato sauce. Prepare the lasagna in a large glass baking dish and cut into serving portions, or stack into a free form individual sculptural masterpiece for each guest.

Zucchini Noodles
2 medium summer squash
3 medium zucchini
¼ cup fresh lemon juice
1 tablespoon extra virgin olive oil
½ teaspoon sea salt

Raw Cashew Cheese (recipe follows)
2 cups baby spinach
1 large Portobello mushroom cap, thinly sliced
Live Tomato Sauce (recipe follows)
½ cup Sprinkle Cheese (page 36)

For the Zucchini Noodles:
1. Cut the ends off the squash, and then cut in half width-wise.

2. Slice as thin as possible length-wise, using knife or mandoline.

3. In a bowl, mix together the lemon juice, olive oil and salt.

4. Place the squash strips in the lemon-oil marinade and set aside.

To Assemble the Lasagna:
1. Drain the squash and blot dry with a clean towel.

2. Lightly oil an 8" x 8" square baking dish.

3. Arrange the squash "noodles" neatly along the bottom of the dish.

4. Spread half of the cashew cheese evenly over the noodles.

5. Arrange spinach leaves and mushroom slices evenly over top and press into cheese.

6. Spoon ⅓ of the tomato sauce over the spinach and mushrooms.

7. Arrange another layer of squash noodles over the top and repeat the cheese, mushroom spinach, tomato sauce layers.

8. Arrange the final layer of noodles, top with tomato sauce, and sprinkle with sprinkle cheese.

Raw Cashew Cheese

Yield: 2 cups

2 cups raw cashews
4 cups water
1 clove garlic, chopped
½ cup nutritional yeast
2 teaspoons fresh lemon juice
½ teaspoon sea salt
pinch fresh ground black pepper
½ teaspoon nama shoyu

1. Soak raw cashews for 20 minutes in water
2. Drain and rinse the cashews.
3. In a food processor, blend the cashews and ½ cup water until creamy.
4. Add garlic and yeast and blend well, pausing to scrape down the sides of the processor container.
5. Add the remaining ingredients and mix well, pausing to scrape down the sides

This will keep for 4 days refrigerated.

Live Tomato Sauce

Yield: 2 cups

1 cup sun-dried tomatoes
1 small tomato, seeded and chopped
½ teaspoon Italian seasoning
¼ cup nutritional yeast
¼ cup extra virgin olive oil
¾ teaspoon sea salt
2 teaspoons fresh lemon juice

1. Soak the sun-dried tomatoes in ¾ cup of warm water for 20 minutes.
2. In a food processor or blender, blend sun-dried tomatoes and water in which they have soaked until smooth.
3. Add the remaining ingredients and blend well, pausing occasionally to scrape down the sides of the blender until mixture is smooth

This will keep for 4 days refrigerated.

Live Nachos

Serves 6-8

These zesty Nachos are great as a starter or as a whole entrée. You won't believe that this simple blend of ingredients can make something so outrageous. A blend of cashews, parsley and nutritional yeast creates the smooth texture of the topper.

1 cup Live Salsa (page 112)

For the Nacho Chips
1½ cups raw sunflower seeds
2 cups ground flax seeds
½ cup ground sesame seeds
1 tablespoon taco seasoning mix
1 tablespoon ground cumin
½ teaspoon sea salt
2 tablespoons nama shoyu
¼ cup minced fresh cilantro
½ cup fresh lime juice
½ cup nutritional yeast
3 scallions, thinly sliced
2 teaspoons minced fresh oregano
1 large jalapeño, seeded and minced

For the Raw Sour Cream
¾ cup raw cashews
⅓ cup fresh lemon juice
2 tablespoons apple cider vinegar
½ teaspoon sea salt
¼ cup chopped fresh parsley
2 tablespoons water

To make the Chips:
1. Soak sunflower seeds for 2 hours in enough water to cover.

2. Drain and rinse the sunflower seeds, then purée in a food processor.

3. Add the flax and sesame to the food processor with all the remaining Nacho Chip ingredients. Process until the mixture becomes a slurry, adding a little water as needed to make it a spreadable consistency.

4. Spread thinly onto Teflex dehydrator sheets. Score into chips roughly 2" x 3" rectangles and dehydrate for 8 hours at 115°. Gently peel chips, flip over, and return to dehydrator until crunchy, about 4 hours.

To make the Raw Sour Cream:
1. Soak the cashews in 2 cups water for 1 hour. Drain and rinse well.

2. Blend the cashews and all the remaining ingredients in a blender or food processor to a smooth cream.

To assemble the Nachos:
Place the chips on a plate, cover with salsa, and top with sour cream

Extra chips can be stored in an airtight container for about 3 weeks or can be frozen for up to 2 months.

Live Pizza Crackers (photo page 124)

Serves 4
These lively fun crackers, made of pumpkin seeds, buckwheat, sunflower seeds, sun-dried tomatoes, carrots, Italian herbs and spices, can be a filling meal in themselves or a great starter. At the restaurant we top these with cashew cheese, sun-dried tomato sauce, dark greens marinated in olive oil and spiral cut yams or zucchini, finished with a tiny bit of sun-dried black olives and the indispensable Sprinkle Cheese.

Raw Pizza Crackers
1 cup ground flax seeds
1 cup buckwheat groats
1 cup raw pumpkin seeds
1 cup raw sunflower seeds
1 cup chopped carrots
2 cups chopped sun-dried tomatoes
½ cup raw sesame seeds
1½ teaspoons dried thyme
1½ teaspoons dried basil
1½ teaspoons garlic powder
1½ teaspoons onion powder
3 cups water
1 teaspoon sea salt

Marinated Greens
2 tablespoons apple cider vinegar
1 tablespoon extra virgin olive oil
¼ teaspoon sea salt
3 leaves kale or dark green of choice, washed and chopped fine

---

2 tablespoons Sprinkle Cheese (page 36)
2 cups Live Tomato Sauce (page 109)
1 cup Raw Cashew Cheese (page 109)
½ cup grated or spiralized zucchini
6 sun-dried black olives, chopped

Make the crackers:
1. Combine all the cracker ingredients, cover with water and allow liquid to absorb.

2. Run mixture through any masticating juicer or process in food processor until mostly smooth with some texture.

3. Spread mixture thinly onto Teflex dehydrator sheet and score crackers into 2"x2" squares. Place in dehydrator at 115° for 8 hours.

4. Flip over and continue to dehydrate for an additional 4-6 hours, until crackers are crunchy.

Assemble the Pizza Crackers:
1. Whisk together the vinegar, oil and salt. Pour over the greens and let marinate for 10 or more minutes.

2. Lay out the crackers and top each with 1 teaspoon of Live Tomato Sauce and 2 teaspoon of Raw Cashew Cheese.

3. Top each cracker with a generous sprinkling of kale, some grated zucchini, roughly 1 teaspoon black olives. Finish with Sprinkle Cheese.

The crackers can be stored in an airtight container for several weeks and are an appetizing addition to any salad.

Chef's Tip:
These pizza crackers should not be assembled too far in advance or they will become soggy.

LIVE FOODS

Live Salsa

Yield: 5 cups

A delicious, fat-free accompaniment to our nachos, live nachos and potato skins. A fresh jalapeño will add fire.

4 medium ripe tomatoes, diced
10 cloves garlic, minced
1 small red onion, minced
1 small white onion, minced
3 scallions, minced
¼ cup finely chopped fresh cilantro
¼ cup fresh lime juice
¼ cup apple cider vinegar
1 teaspoon agave syrup
¾ teaspoon sea salt
½ teaspoon black pepper
pinch cayenne
½ medium jalapeño, minced (optional)

Variations:
Add 1 cup diced fresh pineapple
or 1 cup fresh corn
or 1 cup diced jicama

1. Mix all ingredients together and allow the flavors to marry.

Raw Cheese Trio

Serves 4-6

This is a trio like no other: Smokey Cashew Pecan Cheese, Soft Pumpkin Seed Herb Cheese, and Brazil Nut Tomato Fennel Cheese. Serve these on a bed of baby field greens with golden Flax Crackers, fresh apple slices and grapes for a mouth-watering culinary creation.

Smokey Cashew Pecan Garlic Cheese

1 cup raw pecans, soaked overnight
⅔ cup raw cashews, soaked overnight
½ teaspoon curry powder
1 teaspoon umeboshi plum paste
2 cloves garlic, minced
1 tablespoon water
1 tablespoon extra virgin olive oil
½ teaspoon agave
⅛ teaspoon sea salt
⅛ teaspoon dulse
¼ cup raw pecans, chopped for garnish

Brazil Nut Pumpkin Seed Herb Cheese

3 cups raw pumpkin seed, soaked overnight
1 cup Brazil nuts, soaked overnight
½ cup raw cashews, soaked overnight
¾ cup extra virgin olive oil
¼ cup water
1 tablespoon chopped fresh savory
1 tablespoon chopped fresh sage
2 tablespoons chopped fresh parsley
½ cup chopped fresh dill
2 cloves garlic
2 tablespoons umeboshi plum paste

Cashew Brazil Sun-dried Tomato Fennel Cheese

3 cups raw cashews, soaked overnight
1½ cups Brazil nuts, soaked overnight
½ cup oil
1 cup sun-dried tomatoes, soaked overnight, reserve soaking water
¼ cup nutritional yeast
¼ medium yellow onion
½ teaspoon fennel seeds
1 tablespoon umeboshi plum paste
2 tablespoons agave
2 tablespoons chopped scallion

Flax Crackers (page 106)

To prepare the Smokey Cashew Pecan Garlic Cheese:

1. Drain and rinse both nuts. Transfer nuts to a food processor and process until the mixture forms a paste.

2. Add curry, umeboshi paste, garlic, water, oil and agave and blend until smooth.

3. Add the salt and dulse and mix to incorporate.

4. Chill the mixture. Form into ping-pong sized balls, then flatten and form into wheels and coat them with the chopped pecans.

To prepare the Brazil Nut Pumpkin Seed Herb Cheese:

1. Drain and rinse the seeds and nuts. Transfer them to a food processor and process until the mixture forms a paste.

2. Add oil, water, herbs, garlic, and umeboshi paste, and blend until smooth.

3. Chill the mixture. Form into wheels, as above.

To prepare the Cashew Brazil Sun-Dried Tomato Fennel Cheese:

1. Drain and rinse both nuts. Transfer nuts to a food processor and process the mixture until it forms a paste.

2. Add oil, sun-dried tomatoes, yeast, onion, fennel seeds, umeboshi paste, and agave, and blend, gradually adding reserved soaking water until smooth.

3. Chill, form into small wheels, as described above, and coat them with the chopped scallions.

Raw Herb Vegetable Croquette

Serves 7   Yield: 28 croquettes

A blend of sunflower seeds, pumpkin seeds, carrots, cilantro and spices slowly dehydrated to create a crisp patty, this croquette is packed with calcium, zinc, and beta-carotene, plus savory herbs that help cleanse and detoxify the blood. When we serve these croquettes at the restaurant, we top them with our creamy cashew aioli and serve it over a bed of greens. You can also serve the croquettes on pizza crackers with lettuce and fresh tomato for an on-the-go sandwich.

1 cup raw walnuts
1 cup raw sunflower seeds
1 cup raw pumpkin seeds
1 cup broccoli
1 cup carrots
½ cup diced red onion, rinsed
2 cloves garlic, chopped
¼ cup chopped fresh parsley
¼ cup chopped fresh cilantro
1 tablespoon chopped fresh oregano
2 tablespoons fennel seeds
1 teaspoon black pepper
1 lemon, juiced
3 tablespoons extra virgin olive oil
2 teaspoons sea salt
2 teaspoons miso
Spring greens, for serving

Raw Cashew Aioli (recipe follows)

1. Soak sunflower and pumpkin seeds together in 5 cups water for 2 hours. Drain and rinse well.

2. In a food processor, finely chop the broccoli, carrots, onion, garlic, parsley and cilantro.

3. Add the fennel seeds, oregano and black pepper.

4. Add in the olive oil, salt, lemon juice and soaked seeds and process, scraping down the sides with a rubber spatula as needed to create a smooth mixture.

5. To form croquettes, measure out ¼ cup of mixture, place on a nonstick dehydrator sheet and press down gently.

6. Dehydrate at 115° for 12-16 hours, flipping croquettes over halfway through.

7. Serve on a bed of spring greens, three croquettes per plate, drizzled with the Raw Cashew Aioli.

These croquettes will keep well, refrigerated, for up to a week and can be frozen in an airtight container for 2 months.

Raw Cashew Aioli

Yield: 1½ cups

This creamy sauce is rich and velvety smooth and goes well with the croquettes. Thin it out a bit with water to use as a raw Alfredo sauce over spagetti sliced zucchini or as a delicious dip for any vegetables.

1 cup raw cashews, soaked overnight
½ cup water
1 clove garlic
¼ teaspoon sea salt
⅛ teaspoon dried marjoram
3 tablespoons extra virgin olive oil
1½ teaspoons chopped scallion
½ teaspoon umeboshi plum paste
½ teaspoon nutritional yeast

1. Drain and rinse cashews.

2. Blend all ingredients together in blender until smooth.

You can create a raw noodle entrée by spiralizing a zucchini or summer squash, tossing in this Aioli, and topping with Sprinkle Cheese for a nice finish.

Raw Maki Hand Roll

(photo page 124)

Serves 8

Crisp nori filled with creamy Brazil pumpkin seed nut pâté layered with spinach, thin strips of carrots, zucchini, and shredded cabbage. Feel free to use any seasonal fresh vegetables. Serve with zesty wasabi-miso dressing.

Brazil Nut Pâté
Yield: 1½ cups
¾ cup raw pumpkin seeds, soaked overnight
¾ cup Brazil nuts, soaked overnight
1 clove garlic
2 tablespoons flax oil
½ cup water
pinch cayenne pepper
½ medium lemon, juice and zest
¼ teaspoon sea salt

Miso-Wasabi Dip
Yield: 2 cups
¼ cup miso
1½ cups warm water
1 teaspoon ground ginger
½ cup wasabi powder
2 tablespoons mirin
1 tablespoon black sesame seeds

---

4 sheets nori
1 medium carrot, cut in matchsticks
1 medium avocado, sliced
8 sweet pea shoots
10 spinach leaves, chopped

Prepare the Brazil Nut Pâté:
1. Drain and rinse the pumpkin seeds and the Brazil nuts. Blend garlic, pumpkin seeds and Brazil nuts in food processor until finely ground.
2. Add oil and water to processor and blend until mixture is smooth.
3. Add cayenne, lemon juice and zest and salt and blend for at least 2-3 minutes until smooth.

Prepare the Miso-Wasabi Dip:
1. Blend all dip ingredients except the sesame seeds in a blender.
2. Stir in the sesame seeds.

Assemble the Maki Hand Rolls:
1. Cut the nori sheets in half.
2. Lay a sheet lengthwise in front of you.
3. Smear 1 tablespoon of the pâté on an angle from the bottom center of the nori sheet to the top left-hand corner.
4. Lay out cut vegetables along the smear.
5. Fold the bottom left corner over the ingredients toward the top center and tuck under the ingredients.
6. Roll the sheet toward the center right edge.
7. Moisten the bottom right-hand corner to seal. Repeat

Live Buckwheat Hemp Seed Granola Crunch

Yield: 5 cups

This nutty crunchy granola is full of enzymes and a great way to get the good fats from hemp seeds and sunflower seeds. You can add any fruit to this recipe; just remember to dehydrate for a few hours longer as fresh fruit has higher water content. Dried fruit works very well and the addition of Goji berries, an antioxidant rich dried red berry from Tibet, will give this an extra nutritional punch. Once dehydrated, the granola will keep well in an airtight container for well over a week.

2 cups raw buckwheat groats
2 cups hemp seeds
1 cup raw sunflower seeds
½ cup dates
½ cup water
¼ cup raw agave nectar
½ teaspoon sea salt
1 teaspoon cinnamon
¼ teaspoon nutmeg

1. Rinse the buckwheat groats, then soak in 8 cups of water for 3 hours. Drain and rinse well in a colander until the water runs clear.

2. Allow to drain well, let sit a few minutes, then pat dry with a clean towel.

3. Transfer the buckwheat groats to a large bowl and mix in the hemp seeds and sunflower seeds.

4. In a blender, blend the dates and water together. Add the agave, salt, cinnamon and nutmeg; blend well.

5. Pour the spiced date mixture over the seed mixture and mix in.

6. Spread out thinly onto a Teflex dehydrating sheet and place in a dehydrator at 115° for 12 hours or until dry.

Bliss Cup

Serves 4
An impressive raw dessert that is both rich and healthful.

Carob Mousse
½ cup pitted dates, soaked in 1 cup water
1 tablespoon non-alcoholic vanilla extract
　or ¼ vanilla bean, scraped
3 ripe avocados, mashed
¾ cup carob powder, raw, not roasted
¼ teaspoon sea salt

Vanilla Cashew Cream
1 cup raw cashews,
　soaked in 2 cups water
6 pitted dates, soaked in ½ cup water
1 tablespoon non-alcoholic vanilla extract
　or ¼ vanilla bean, scraped
¼ teaspoon sea salt

Raspberry Topping
1 pint fresh raspberries, or a 10-ounce
　bag frozen raspberries, defrosted
1 tablespoon agave syrup
mint leaves for garnish

To make the mousse:
1. Drain the dates, reserving the soaking water.
2. In a food processor, blend the dates, vanilla, and salt until smooth.
3. Add the avocado and process until smooth.
4. Add the carob powder and 1-2 tablespoons of the date soaking water and blend until smooth.

To make the cream:
1. Drain the cashews and discard the soaking water.
2. Add the drained cashews, the dates and their soaking water, the vanilla extract and sea salt to a blender and blend until smooth.

To assemble the Bliss:
1. Spoon ½ cup of the mousse into the bottom of each of 4 sundae or wine glasses.
2. Mix the raspberries with the agave necter.
3. Spoon ¼ cup of the raspberries onto the mousse in each cup and top each with ¼ cup of the vanilla cream.
4. Repeat the procedure, layering the remaining mousse, berries and vanilla cream, then garnish with fresh mint leaves and serve.

Top with some chopped pecans for added crunch!

Nell's Coconut Rolls

Yield: 50 rolls

When Nell worked at Down to Earth, she loved anything with a tropical flair - and her coconut date rolls are no exception. A simple, sweet, decadent treat that is perfect for a bag lunch, picnic or as an afternoon pick me up.

8 ounces raw almonds, about 1⅓ cups
½ teaspoon sea salt
1 teaspoon cinnamon
2 cups pitted dates
2 tablespoons fresh lemon juice
¼ cup coconut milk
1 cup unsweetened shredded coconut meat
1 tablespoon cinnamon, for sprinkling

1. Process the almonds in a food processor to a sandy consistency and transfer to a medium bowl.

2. Add the salt and cinnamon to the bowl and whisk to combine.

3. Process the dates in a food processor until smooth, scraping down the sides of the container as needed.

4. Add the processed dates, the lemon juice and coconut milk to the almond mixture and stir to combine.

5. Scoop the mixture out in teaspoons and roll into balls.

6. Roll the balls in shredded coconut and sprinkle with cinnamon.

Raw Apple Pie

Serves 8 **Yield: 1 9" pie**

Guilt-free goodness even macrobiotic and diabetic people can enjoy. A filling of sliced apples, medjool dates, and spices is piled high in a dehydrated pecan crust. Top with rich and creamy cashew whipped cream.

Raw Pecan Crust
2 cups pecans
6 dates, pitted
1 tablespoon raw agave nectar
1 tablespoon flax oil
1 teaspoon cinnamon
½ teaspoon freshly ground nutmeg
1 tablespoon non-alcoholic vanilla extract
½ teaspoon sea salt

Apple Filling
8 pitted dates
4 medium apples, peeled, cored and sliced thin
⅛ teaspoon nutmeg
½ teaspoon cinnamon
¼ cup raisins
1 lemon, zested and juiced

1 cup Raw Cream Whip Topping (recipe follows)

Serve with Raw Cream Whip Topping.

Lightly oil a 9" pie plate and set aside.

Make the crust:
1. Soak the pecans in 2 cups water and the dates in ½ cup water for half an hour. Drain and rinse both well.

2. In a food processor, chop the pecans into a fine meal and set aside.

3. Put the soaked dates into the processor and chop. Add the chopped nuts, agave, oil, spices, vanilla and salt, and process until the mixture is sticky enough to hold shape when pressed in, but not too wet.

4. Transfer the mixture to the prepared pie plate and press the crust evenly up to the rim of the plate.

5. If a crisper crust is desired, dehydrate at 115° for approximately 6 hours.

Make the filling:
1. Soak the dates in 3 cups water for 30-40 minutes or until soft. Drain, reserving the soaking water.

2. In a food processor, blend the dates using the soaking water as needed to produce a smooth mixture.

3. Pour the date mixture into a large sized mixing bowl. Add the apples, nutmeg, cinnamon, raisins, lemon zest and juice with the mixture, and mix well.

4. Fill the pie crust with the mixture and chill.

Raw Cream Whip Topping

Yield: 1 cup

A rich and smooth sweet topper for all your topping needs.

1 cup raw cashews
6 pitted dates
1 tablespoon raw agave nectar
2 tablespoons extra virgin olive oil
1 tablespoon non-alcoholic vanilla extract
¼ teaspoon sea salt

1. Soak the cashews in 2 cups water for 30-40 minutes. Drain and rinse well.

2. Soak the dates in 1 cup warm water until soft. Drain reserving soaking water.

3. Place in a blender the cashews, dates, agave, oil, vanilla and salt, and blend, adding the date soaking water as needed until a smooth tahini-like consistency has been achieved.

Raw Lemon Pie

Serves 8   Yield: 1 9" pie

The rich blend of cashews, agave syrup, and fresh lemon juice will satisfy your sweet cravings without all of the refined sugars. Enjoy topped with fresh fruit for an extra treat.

Raw Brazil Nut Crust
1 cup Brazil nuts
3 dried pineapple rings
6 pitted dates
1 cup coconut flakes
1 tablespoon raw agave nectar
1 tablespoon flax oil
1 tablespoon cinnamon
1 teaspoon freshly ground nutmeg
1 tablespoon non-alcoholic vanilla extract
½ teaspoon sea salt

Lemon Cream Filling
2 cups raw cashews
1 cup pitted dates
½ teaspoon sea salt
¼ cup raw agave nectar
¼ cup fresh lemon juice
2 tablespoons non-alcoholic vanilla extract

Lightly oil a 9" pie plate and set aside.

Make the pie crust:
1. Soak the Brazil nuts in 1 cup water, the pineapple rings in 1 cup water and the dates in ½ cup water for half an hour. Drain all and rinse well.

2. Place the drained nuts in a food processor, and process into a fine meal. Set aside.

3. Put the soaked pineapple, dates, and coconut into the processor and chop. Add the chopped nuts, agave, oil, spices, vanilla and salt; mix well.

4. The mixture should be sticky enough to hold its shape when pressed in, but not too wet.

5. Press the crust evenly into the pie plate up to the rim.

6. If a crisper crust is desired, dehydrate at 115° for approximately 6 hours.

Make the filling:
1. Soak the cashews in 3 cups water for half an hour. Drain and repeat for another half hour.

2. Soak the dates in 1 cup warm water for 20 minutes to soften.

3. Drain both, reserving date soaking water, and rinse well.

4. Combine all the filling ingredients in a blender or food processor and blend well. Scrape down the sides as needed until smooth and creamy. Add the date soaking water as necessary.

5. Fill the pie crust with the filling and chill in the refrigerator to set.

Chickpea Socca
Recipe on page 134

Above:
Live Pizza Crackers
Recipe on page 111

Left:
Raw Maki Hand Roll
Recipe on page 116

Right:
Leaf Wraps
Recipe on page 107

Blue Corn Hempeh
Recipe on page 132

Tiffany's Pancakes
Recipe on page 173

Facing Page Top:
Gado Gado
Recipe on page 80

Facing Page Bottom:
Seitan Saty
Recipe on page 144

Left:
Magic Cookies and Root Beer Float
Magic Cookies Recipe on page 178
Root Beer Float Recipe on page 157

Below:
Rainforest Crunch
Recipe on page 194-195

Chocolate Ganache Cake
Recipe on page 188

Entrées

When regular clients come to Down to Earth, they often bring along guests who have never been to an all-vegan restaurant. We frequently get questions like "where's the beef?" and "can I get a burger or a steak?"

However, once these newcomers have seen and had a chance to sample the many appealing, varied and delicious menu choices they usually respond "Wow ~ we can't wait to come back!" Our main courses are created around wholesome ingredients such as grains and beans, and ancient, traditional soy foods like miso, tempeh and tofu. Another high-protein staple is seitan, an especially popular alternative made from the gluten in wheat. The Seitan Satay, with its grilled juiciness and spicy peanut sauce, is delicious. Customers tell us it's flavor is addictive.

Chickpea Socca, another dish we have had since our opening, is a pleasing wheat-free option of chickpea cakes served with leeks cooked to perfection and tender greens.

Like traditional meat-based dishes, these entrées form the centerpiece of a meal, with an array of starters and desserts playing supporting roles. Some of these recipes take a little longer to prepare but you'll find they're worth the effort. Using healthful, organically grown ingredients makes beautiful and satisfying dishes every time. We find when diners try these inventive dishes, free of harmful chemicals and hormones, even die-hard meat eaters' minds can be changed forever.

Blue Corn Hempeh (photo page 126)

Serves 4

A long-time favorite at the restaurant and a great introduction to eating tempeh. The marinated tempeh is coated with hemp seeds, cornmeal, and crunchy blue corn chips, then topped off with a zesty mustard sauce. We serve it accompanied by mashed potatoes, Mushroom Gravy, Sautéed Greens and a southern classic, Tomato Pudding, all stacked into a comfort food tower.

Yellow Mustard Sauce
¼ cup olive oil
1 medium onion, chopped
5 cloves garlic, minced
½ teaspoon paprika
½ teaspoon turmeric
¼ teaspoon sea salt
1 tablespoon drained capers
¼ cup yellow mustard
⅓ cup water
½ of one 12.3-ounce box Silken Lite Tofu

Dredge
2 cups crushed blue corn tortilla chips
½ cup hemp seeds
½ cup unbleached flour
1 cup whole-grain cornmeal
1½ teaspoons paprika
1 teaspoon dried thyme
1 cup unsweetened soymilk
2 tablespoons Dijon mustard

8 ounces Marinated Tempeh (page 28)

¾ cup conola or other flavorless oil
Tomato Pudding (recipe follows)
Mashed Potatoes (page 38)
Mushroom Gravy (page 33)
Sautéed Greens (page 42)

Prepare the Mustard Sauce:
1. Sauté onion and garlic in oil. When the onion is translucent, add paprika, turmeric and sea salt, and continue to sauté until onions are soft.
2. Place the onion mixture in a blender with the remaining sauce ingredients and blend until smooth.

Prepare the dredge:
1. Process chips and hemp seeds in a food processor until finely ground.
2. Add the remaining dredge ingredients, except the soymilk and the mustard.
3. Set aside in a bowl or on a baking sheet.
4. Whisk together the soymilk and mustard and set aside in a shallow bowl.

Prepare the Tempeh:
1. Cut the marinated tempeh in half lengthwise.
2. Dredge the tempeh slices first in soymilk mixture, shaking off excess, then in dry mixture, covering completely.
3. In a large skillet, heat the canola oil over medium-high heat to 350° or until a small piece of hempeh coating dropped into the oil floats to the top and bubbles.
4. Fry slices until golden and crispy, flipping halfway through.
5. Drain on paper towels and serve with yellow mustard sauce, accompanied by tomato pudding, mashed potatoes and mushroom gravy and sautéed greens.

Tomato Pudding

Serves 6

This is a vegan version of a southern classic. We use it as a component to the Blue Corn Hempeh, but it is sweet and fabulous on its own.

26 ounces canned diced tomatoes, drained
2 cups cubed bread
¼ cup coconut oil or vegan margarine
¼ cup molasses
¼ cup Sucanat
1 tablespoon extra virgin olive oil
1 teaspoon sea salt
2 pinches black pepper

Preheat oven to 375°

1. Mix together all ingredients.

2. Pour the mixture into an ungreased 9 x 13" baking dish and bake for 45 minutes or until the edges are brown and bubbling.

Chickpea Socca (photo page 123)

Serves 4

We've elevated the traditional Mediterranean street food to a more formal and healthier level. Served with sautéed dark greens and garlicky white beans, this wheat-free dish is satisfying and nutritious.

Caramelized Leeks
2 teaspoons extra virgin olive oil
2 medium leeks, well-washed and sliced thin
½ teaspoon sea salt

Socca
2 cups chickpea flour
¼ teaspoon sea salt
2 tablespoons herbes de Provence
3 cups warm water
1 cup extra virgin olive oil

House Marinara (page 32)
Sautéed Greens (page 42)

White Bean Purée
2 cups cooked white beans or 1 15-ounce can, drained and rinsed
½ cup minced fresh parsley
6 cloves roasted garlic
3 tablespoons extra virgin olive oil, or as needed
¼ teaspoon sea salt

Prepare the White Bean Purée:
1. In a blender or food processor, blend beans, parsley and garlic together.
2. Add enough oil to achieve a rich and creamy consistency.
3. Add sea salt to taste.

Prepare the Caramelized Leeks:
1. Heat the oil in a sauté pan over medium-low heat.
2. Add the leeks and the salt and cook, stirring often until the leeks begin to caramelize and turn a golden brown, about 10-15 minutes. Remove from heat and set aside.

Prepare the Socca:
1. Combine the chickpea flour, salt and herbs.
2. Add water and whisk until smooth.
3. Whisk in oil, cover and allow to rest 1 hour.
4. Preheat oven to 450°.
5. Grease a 9"x13" baking dish with oil and heat in the oven for 2 minutes.
6. Take pan out of the oven, re whisk batter and pour into the hot pan.
7. Return the pan to the oven and bake 12-15 minutes until socca is set and starts to crisp.
8. Remove from the oven and score the socca into 12 roughly 3"x 3" pieces. You will need 3 slices for each serving.

To assemble Socca:
1. Spoon a couple tablespoons of marinara onto a plate and place a piece of socca on top.
2. Put 2 tablespoons of white bean purée on the socca slice and top with sautéed greens.
3. Place the next piece of socca, on top of the bean purée and top with the greens.
4. Add the third slice of socca. Top with 1 tablespoon bean purée, a tablespoon of House Marinara and the caramelized leeks.

Hijiki Sea Cakes

Serves 4-6

These wholesome and delicious cakes are swimming with minerals from the sea. We top them with our version of a classic creamy tartar sauce that even people who never thought they liked tartar sauce will love.

1 14-ounce block firm tofu, drained
¼ cup dry hijiki seaweed,
    soaked in 4 cups water
½ medium onion, finely diced
3 cloves garlic, sliced
pinch of cayenne pepper
1½ teaspoons dried dill
1 teaspoon dried thyme
1½ teaspoons Spike
1 tablespoon broth powder
    or ½ vegan bouillon cube
1½ teaspoons lemon juice
2 tablespoons mirin
1 tablespoon chopped scallion
1 tablespoon chopped fresh parsley
    or 1 teaspoon dried
½ cup bread crumbs

Tartar Sauce
5 small dill pickles, diced small
1 tablespoon minced red onion
1¼ teaspoons Spike
1½ teaspoons lemon zest
1 scallion, sliced
1 teaspoon chopped fresh parsley
    or ¼ teaspoon dried
¾ cup Vegenaise
1 small clove garlic
¾ teaspoon mustard
¾ teaspoon lemon juice
¼ teaspoon Florida Crystals

1 lemon for garnish

Preheat the oven to 350°.

1. Crumble the tofu into a food processor.

2. Pulse in the sea vegetables.

3. Sauté the onion and garlic until soft.

4. Add the herbs, spices and broth powder to the pan and cook for 2 minutes. Then add to the tofu mixture, pulsing until just combined.

5. Mix the lemon juice and mirin, deglaze the pan and add its contents to the tofu mixture.

6. Process the tofu mixture in a food processor until smooth.

7. Add the bread crumbs, chopped scallion and parsley, and mix well.

8. Form the mixture into golf-ball size cakes, flatten slightly, and place on a baking sheet lined with parchment paper. Bake for 15 minutes.

9. Meanwhile, to prepare the tartar sauce, mix all the sauce ingredients together in a bowl.

Serve the cakes on a plate dressed with lemon wedges and a small side of the tartar sauce.

Herbed Tofu Loaf with Apple Herb Stuffing and Cranberry Orange Relish

Serves 4

This tofu loaf makes a great holiday entrée. We have served it to countless happy customers for many Thanksgivings, and now you can enjoy it at home. The moist, herbal stuffing gets its tart kick from the apple and its nutty crunch from the walnuts. It will remind you of the savory stuffings of Thanksgivings past without any of the poultry. And what Thanksgiving feast would be complete without cranberry relish? Here's our version.

Cranberry Orange Relish
1½ cups cranberries, fresh or frozen
1 cup maple syrup
1 cup orange juice
1 medium orange, zested
1 medium lemon, zested and juiced
pinch sea salt

Apple and Herb Bread Stuffing
3 tablespoons extra virgin olive oil
1 medium tart apple, peeled, cored and diced
½ small white onion, minced
2 ribs celery, cut in ¼ inch cubes
2 cloves garlic, minced
1 teaspoon dried thyme
1 teaspoon dried sage
1 teaspoon dried basil
4 cups stale bread, cubed
¼ cup stock
¼ teaspoon black pepper, or to taste
sea salt, to taste

Herbed Tofu Loaf (recipe follows)

Prepare the Cranberry Orange Relish:
1. In a medium sauce pan over medium-high heat, combine the cranberries, maple syrup, citrus juices and zests, and bring to a boil.

2. Lower the heat and cook until the cranberries pop, approximately 10 minutes.

3. Add the salt and remove from the heat.

4. Chill and serve. If a cranberry sauce is desired, blend in a blender or food processor until smooth.

Prepare the Stuffing
1. In a medium pot, sauté onion, apple, celery and garlic in oil.

2. Add herbs to sauté and mix well.

3. Stir bread into mixture and pour in stock.

4. Mix all together well until moist.

5. Add salt and pepper to taste.

Herbed Tofu Loaf

Herbed Tofu Loaf
2 14-ounce blocks firm tofu, drained
3 tablespoons extra virgin olive oil
1 medium onion, cut in medium dice
2 cloves garlic, minced
¾ cup nutritional yeast
3 tablespoons tamari
⅛ teaspoon black pepper
1 tablespoon dried thyme
1 tablespoon dried basil
2¼ cups Italian bread crumbs
1 tablespoon white miso

Preheat the oven to 350°. Oil a loaf pan and line it with parchment. Set aside.

Prepare the Tofu Loaf
1. In a medium bowl, mash the tofu.

2. Heat the oil in a pan and sauté the onions and garlic until soft.

3. Add the sautéed garlic, onion, and the remaining loaf ingredients to the tofu and combine well in food processor.

5. Divide the mixture in half and spread one half in the bottom of the pan, pressing down firmly with a spoon.

6. Spread ½ cup of the stuffing evenly over the tofu layer and top with the remaining tofu.

7. Oil the top of the loaf and bake 25-30 minutes or until firm to the touch.

8. Allow the loaf to cool 10 minutes, then turn out and serve sliced.

Serve with Mushroom Gravy (page 33)

Kevin's Tofu Murphy

Serves 4

Like a classic song that always gets you going, this dish will rock your taste buds. Kevin's version of the traditional Murphy will have you screaming encore!

1 14-ounce block extra-firm tofu, drained
2 tablespoons extra virgin olive oil, for coating
3 medium Yukon Gold potatoes, quartered
¼ cup extra virgin olive oil
1 large sweet onion, chopped
1 medium red pepper, chopped
1 medium green pepper, chopped
1 medium yellow pepper, chopped
10 cloves garlic, minced
2 medium Portobello mushrooms, sliced
10 cherry peppers
2 teaspoons dried oregano
¼ teaspoon red pepper flakes (optional)
salt and pepper, to taste
1 cup vegetable stock

Preheat the oven to 350°.

1. Cut the tofu into bite-sized cubes, lightly coat with olive oil, and bake for 10-15 minutes until golden brown.

2. In a large sauté pan, sauté the potatoes in the ¼ cup of the olive oil over medium heat for 10 minutes.

3. Add the onion, red, green and yellow peppers, garlic and mushroom slices to the pan. Cook for 5 minutes.

4. Add the baked tofu, cherry peppers, oregano, red pepper flakes (if using), salt, pepper, and vegetable stock. Simmer for 10 minutes or until the potatoes are fork tender.

Love Bowl

Serves 1

Our signature Love Bowl is a hearty comfort food at its best. Enjoy!

1 cup cooked brown rice
2 cup cooked black beans or
   1 15-ounce can, drained and rinsed
1 cup Sautéed Greens (page 42)
4 ounces Marinated Tempeh (page 28) or
4 slabs Baked Tofu, cut in half diagonally
   (page 26)
3 cup of the sauce of your choice:
   Peanut Sauce (page 34),
   or Mushroom Gravy (page 33)
Toasted sesame seeds, for garnish
Thinly sliced scallion, for garnish

1. In a medium serving bowl, put the rice, beans, greens, tempeh or tofu, and top with your favorite sauce.

Serve hot, sprinkled with sesame seeds and scallions.

Pizza

Yield: 2 10" pizzas

With this convenient method for making pizza, you're on the road to pizza freedom. Try one of our suggestions or let your imagination be your guide.

1⅓ cups warm water
1 teaspoon active dry yeast
1 teaspoon Sucanat
3 tablespoons extra virgin olive oil
2 teaspoons sea salt
1 tablespoon Italian seasoning
4 cups unbleached flour

Toppings
Vine ripened tomatoes
   with fresh basil and olive oil
sauteed spinach
blanched broccoli
roasted garlic
   (see Step 1, page 57 for directions)
artichoke hearts
Tofu Cheese (page 36)
House Marinara (page 32)
Tempeh Sausage (page 163)
sauteed zucchini
or any other vegetables you desire

1. In a medium sized bowl, combine the water, yeast and Sucanat and let the mixture rest in warm spot for 5 minutes until it looks foamy.

2. Mix in the olive oil, salt and seasoning.

3. Add flour slowly, stirring until the dough comes together. It should not be too sticky.

4. Turn the dough out onto a lightly floured work surface and knead for 10 minutes until it is smooth and elastic.

5. Coat the inside of a bowl with 2 tablespoons oil and place the dough inside, rolling it to coat all surfaces with oil.

6. Cover the dough with plastic wrap and let the dough rise for at least 12 hours in a warm, draft-free place.

7. Preheat the oven to 450°.

8. Lightly knead the dough and divide in half.

9. Cover one half with a damp towel and shape the other half into a free-form circle.

10. Transfer the formed dough to a baking sheet or pizza stone if you have one and brush the crust with olive oil. Make sure to poke a few holes in the crust. Pre-bake for 3 minutes.

11. Add the topping of your choice and bake in the pre-heated 450° oven for 10 minutes.

12. Prepare and bake the second pizza with the remaining dough.

Coconut Seitan

Serves 4-6

A taste of the islands – pan-fried Brazil nut crusted coconut seitan, topped with a tart/sweet pineapple mango chutney - this dish will make you feel the sun is shining even on the coldest day of the year.

Pineapple Mango Marmalade
1 cup chopped fresh pineapple
½ ripe mango, peeled and diced
½ cup red diced onion
1 tablespoon extra virgin olive oil
½ teaspoon minced fresh sage
 or ¼ teaspoon dried
1 medium roasted red peppers,
 roughly chopped
4 teaspoons agave nectar or rice syrup
1 tablespoon rice vinegar
1½ teaspoons fresh lemon juice
pinch sea salt

Coconut Saitan
Dredge
½ cup Brazil nuts
¾ cup unsweetened grated coconut
¾ cup unbleached flour
½ teaspoon sea salt
pinch black pepper
pinch paprika

Wash
1 cup coconut or soy milk
2 tablespoons Vegenaise

1 pound seitan, sliced ½" thick

1½ cups flavorless oil, for frying

Prepare Pineapple Mango Marmalade:
1. In a 2-3 quart saucepan, place all the marmalade ingredients and cook on medium heat until bubbling.

2. Reduce the heat and continue to stir, cooking for about 15-20 minutes, or until mixture has thickened slightly.

3. Remove from the heat and set aside to cool, letting the flavors marry.

Prepare the Seitan:
1. Grind Brazil nuts in a food processor until crumbly.

2. Add the coconut, flour, salt, pepper and paprika, and pulse for 1 more minute to incorporate.

3. Transfer the mixture to a shallow pan.

Wash:
1. In another shallow pan, whisk together the coconut or soymilk and the Vegenaise.

2. Dip the seitan slices in the wash, then coat each slice thoroughly in the dredge to end up with a fairly dry piece of coated seitan.

3. In a large frying pan, heat the oil over medium high heat until hot. Test by tossing a crumb into the oil - if it bubbles, the oil is ready.

4. Gently slip pieces of seitan in to the oil and cook until golden. Remove and place on paper towels to drain.

Serve with Mashed Coconut Yams (page 39).

Baked Samosas

Serves 4

A lighter version of the Indian classic, these samosas are baked and served as an entrée, crispy without the frying. They're filled with a wonderful medley of spiced potatoes, peas, and onions. The tangy Banana Ginger Chutney makes a wonderful accompaniment.

Samosa Filling
4 cups peeled and diced potatoes
2 tablespoons olive oil
1 small red onion, minced
3 cloves garlic, chopped
½ teaspoon coriander
1½ teaspoons mustard seed
¾ teaspoon cumin
½ teaspoon curry powder
2 tablespoons Sucanat
¼ cup coconut milk
1 tablespoon lime juice
¼ teaspoon black pepper
¾ teaspoon sea salt
½ cup peas, fresh or thawed frozen

4 large whole wheat tortillas

Prepare the Chutney:
　See recipe following Page

Prepare the Samosa filling:
1. Boil the potatoes until soft; drain.

2. Heat the olive oil in a large pot, and cook the onion, garlic, and spices until the onions are soft.

3. Add the Sucanat, coconut milk, and lime juice, and cook 2 minutes more.

4. Mix in the potatoes and black pepper, and cook for 5 minutes more. Add salt.

5. At the end of cooking, add the peas and mix well.

To assemble the Samosas:
Preheat the oven to 425°
1. In the center of each 9" tortilla, place approximately ½ cup of the samosa filling.

2. Fold the sides of each tortilla in towards the center and wrap the bottom up and over to form a rectangle. Cut diagonally across.

3. On an oiled baking sheet, place the samosa halves seam side down and brush the tops with a bit of oil.

4. Bake for 10-15 minutes or until crispy.

While the samosas bake, prepare the Tamarind Sauce:
See recipe following Page

Serve each samosa topped with chutney and tamarind sauce. (recipe follows)

Banana Ginger Chutney and Tamarind Sauce

Banana Ginger Chutney
1½ dried Anaheim chili peppers
3 medium bananas, chopped
½ medium onion, chopped
½ medium apple, chopped small
¼ cup raisins
1 cup apple cider vinegar
¾ cup Sucanat
2 tablespoons minced fresh ginger
1½ tablespoons curry powder
½ medium lime, zested and juiced
½ teaspoon sea salt

Tamarind Sauce
¼ cup tamarind pulp
2¼ teaspoons sea salt
1 teaspoon black pepper
2¼ cups Sucanat
¾ teaspoon cayenne
1½ tablespoons cumin seed, toasted and ground
2 cups water

Banana Ginger Chutney:
1. Rehydrate chilies in hot water and rinse thoroughly to remove seeds.

2. Combine chilies and all other chutney ingredients in a 4-6 quart stock pot.

3. Simmer over medium heat for 20-25 minutes, stirring often to prevent sticking. The chutney will start to darken and thicken.

4. Let cool and use as a condiment. The chutney will keep 3-4 weeks, refrigerated.

Tamarind Sauce:
1. Place all the sauce ingredients in a pot and bring to a boil.

2. Remove from heat and set aside to cool. Serve each samosa topped with chutney and tamarind sauce.

To create a substantial entrée, serve with seasonal vegetables atop Cashew Rice (page 29)

Seitan Satay

(photo page 128)

Serves 6

This Thai-style marinated and grilled seitan served with a spicy peanut sauce has been one of our best sellers at the restaurant for years. Even die-hard carnivores come back for more.

24 wooden skewers,
  soaked in water for 15 minutes

Cilantro Marinade
2 bunches cilantro, washed well
1½ cups canola oil
1 cup rice syrup
¼ cup lemon juice
½ teaspoon salt
½ teaspoon black pepper

6 cups seitan cut in 1" pieces

½ cup Peanut Sauce (page 34)

Preheat a grill and lightly oil.

1. Chop cilantro leaves and stems.

2. Place cilantro and remaining marinade ingredients in a blender and blend well.

3. Skewer seitan pieces a few to a skewer and pour the marinade over the seitan sticks.

4. Place seitan sticks on grill, and grill, turning the skewers carefully once or twice while cooking, until the seitan is cooked through and lightly charred around the edges.

5. Remove the sticks from the grill and drizzle with peanut sauce.

Serve with brown rice and sautéed seasonal vegetables.

Southern Style Seitan

Serves 6

You don't have to live in the South to create fabulous southern-style cuisine. It's the 11 herbs and spices brought together in Cajun spice that really make the flavor of this dish - crisp seitan nuggets served with a tangy Maple Mustard Sauce and sautéed greens.

Maple Mustard Sauce
½ cup stone-ground mustard
3 tablespoons olive oil
4½ teaspoons tamari
½ cup maple syrup
4½ teaspoons water

Seitan
6 cups seitan, torn into nuggets
1½ cups plus 2 tablespoons unbleached flour
¼ cup Cajun spice (page 20)
¾ teaspoon salt and pepper
1½ cups canola oil, for frying

Prepare the Maple Mustard Sauce:
Put all sauce ingredients into a blender, blend until smooth and set aside.

Prepare the Seitan:
1. In a large bowl, coat the seitan nuggets with flour.

2. Add the Cajun spice and re-coat the seitan.

3. Season with salt and pepper.

4. Heat the oil in a large pot and fry the coated seitan nuggets in small batches until crisp.

5. Drain the nuggets on paper towels when done.

6. Sprinkle with more Cajun spice and salt and pepper to taste.

Serve with Maple Mustard Sauce, Sautéed Greens (page 42) and Roasted Yams (page 39).

Thai Coconut Tempeh Stix

Serves 4-6

This dish is inspired by the flavors of Thailand.

Basil Lemongrass Sauce
¼ cup ginger root slices
4 cloves garlic
2 tablespoons fresh basil
4 pieces star anise
3 tablespoons lemongrass
1 15-ounce can coconut milk
1½ cups water
1½ tablespoons broth powder
1½ teaspoons sea salt
3 tablespoons kuzu
⅔ cup water
2 tablespoons rice syrup

Thai Dry Mix
1¼ cups dried bread crumbs
1 cup sesame seeds
¾ cup unsweetened coconut flakes

8 ounces Marinated Tempeh (page 28)

Prepare Basil Lemongrass Sauce:
1. Place ginger, garlic, basil, star anise, and lemon grass in a piece of washed cheesecloth and tie securely.
2. Place the cheesecloth bundle, coconut milk, water, salt, and broth powder in a saucepan, bring to a simmer, and cook for 20 minutes.
3. Remove the cheesecloth bundle and press liquid back into the saucepan through a strainer.
4. Make a kuzu slurry by mixing the kuzu and ⅔ cup water in a small container.
5. Add the slurry and the rice syrup to the saucepan and simmer an additional 10 minutes. Remove from the heat and set aside.
6. Reserve ½ cup of the sauce for dredging.

Prepare Thai dry mix:
In a medium sized bowl, combine the bread crumbs, sesame seeds and coconut flakes.

Prepare Tempeh Stix:
1. Preheat the oven to 375°. Oil a baking sheet and set aside.
2. Cut the marinated tempeh in half and cut each half into three sticks.
3. In one medium size bowl, place ½ cup of the Basil Lemongrass Sauce for dredging liquid; in another, the Thai dry mix.
4. Submerge the tempeh sticks in the dredge liquid, shake off any excess, and roll each of the stix in the dry mix until completely coated.
5. Place the stix on an oiled baking sheet and bake for 15 minutes or until golden.

Serve with the remaining Basil Lemongrass Sauce and Cashew Rice (page 29).

Vegetable Lasagna

Serves 6

From Grandparents to kids, who doesn't love this family favorite? It's easy to prepare in any season, using whatever fresh vegetables the market has to offer. In summer, grill the vegetables for an extra layer of flavor, or try roasted vegetables, such as zucchini and summer squash. This is a good recipe to make ahead. It can also be frozen and is great for a buffet.

3 medium yams
2 tablespoons extra virgin olive oil
1 teaspoon garlic powder
2 packages lasagna noodles
6 cups House Marinara (page 32)
8 ounces baby spinach, washed
3 cups Tofu Cheese (page 36)

Preheat the oven to 350°. Oil a 9"x13" baking dish and set aside. Line a baking sheet with parchment.

1. Peel the yams and cut into bite sized chunks. Place them in a medium sized bowl and toss with oil and garlic powder.

2. Spread the yams out on the parchment-lined baking sheet and bake for 15-20 minutes until soft and golden. Sprinkle with salt and pepper while still hot.

3. While the yams bake, cook the lasagna noodles according to package directions, and drain.

4. When the yams and the noodles are done, begin assembly.

5. Spread 1 cup of House Marinara over the bottom of the baking dish and cover with a layer of 5 overlapping lasagna noodles.

6. Scatter ⅓ of the spinach and ⅓ of the roasted yams over the noodles, then top with ¼ of the tofu cheese.

7. Repeat layering the noodles, spinach, yams and cheese twice more.

8. Pour on 1 cup of marinara, then place last layer of noodles.

9. Mix 1 cup of marinara with the reamaining tofu cheese and spread over the top.

10. Cover with foil and bake for 15 minutes; remove the foil and bake an additional 15 minutes.

11. Remove from the oven and let rest 10 minutes before cutting and serving.

To prepare ahead, simply bake and chill. It reheats well and will keep for 4 days in the refrigerator or 3 to 4 weeks in the freezer. To reheat, thaw, if frozen, cover with foil, and bake in preheated oven at 400° for 15 minutes covered, remove foil and bake another 10 minutes, uncovered.

White Bean Crêpes with Balsamic Grilled Tempeh & Basil Butter

Serves 6

In this recipe we've used white beans for the filling but you can fill this versatile crêpe with your favorite vegetables or fruit compotes.

For the Crêpes
1 cup unbleached flour
3 tablespoons gluten flour
2 teaspoons Sucanat
½ teaspoon sea salt
2 tablespoons canola oil
2 cups water

For the Filling
2 tablespoons extra virgin olive oil
5 cloves garlic, whole
3 cups baby spinach, washed
2 cups cooked white beans
   or 1-15 ounce can, drained and rinsed
½ teaspoon sea salt
pinch black pepper

Balsamic Grilled Tempeh
and Basil Butter (recipes follow)

Make the Crêpes:
1. In a medium bowl, whisk together the dry ingredients.

2. Add the oil and water, and whisk to combine. The batter should be thin.

3. Heat a small amount of oil in a nonstick pan over medium heat.

4. Pour ¼ cup of batter into the center of the pan and swirl to coat the bottom of the pan.

5. When bubbles appear on top and the edges are brown, flip the crêpe and lightly brown the other side. Transfer to a foil-covered plate and repeat with the remaining crêpes. Keep covered crêpes warm in a 250° oven until ready to use.

Prepare the Filling:
1. Sauté the garlic cloves in olive oil over low heat. When the garlic browns, remove from the oil and set aside.

2. Sauté the spinach until wilted, remove from heat and let cool.

3. Chop together the garlic and spinach, mix into the white beans, and add salt and pepper.

Chef's Tip:
Prepare Balsamic Grilled Tempeh before starting the crêpes.

Balsamic Grilled Tempeh & Basil Butter

For the Tempeh
1 teaspoon hot sauce
2 tablespoons extra virgin olive oil
2 tablespoons balsamic vinegar
1 teaspoon dried rosemary
1 teaspoon Italian seasoning
1 tablespoon stone-ground mustard
1 pound tempeh cut in 4 equal pieces

For Basil "Butter"
1 bunch fresh basil
¼ cup vegan margarine
1 tablespoon extra virgin olive oil
½ teaspoon pepper

Prepare the Tempeh:
1. Blend the hot sauce, oil, vinegar, rosemary, seasoning and mustard in a blender until smooth.

2. Pour the mixture over the tempeh pieces and let them marinate 1 hour or more.

3. Oil and preheat a grill. Grill the tempeh on both sides and return it to the marinade. If no grill is available, place tempeh under broiler and broil until slightly charred, flipping once to ensure even browning.

4. When ready to use, cut the tempeh into 12 equal pieces.

Prepare the Basil "Butter":
1. Blanch the basil briefly in salted boiling water, and shock in ice water to brighten the color. Drain well

2. Blend the basil, margarine, oil and pepper in a blender and refrigerate. Serve on the hot crêpes.

To assemble Crêpes:
1. In the center of each crêpe, place a generous ¼ cup scoop of the white bean filling.

2. Roll each crêpe. Place 3 filled crêpes on each plate and place 2 pieces of grilled tempeh over them. Drizzle with Basil "Butter" and serve hot.

Serve with Roasted Tomato, Basil and Corn Salad (page 88).

Wild Rice Risotto Cakes

Serves 4

The wild rice adds a pleasing crunch to these risotto cakes, and the brown rice makes them exceptionally nutritious. Serve these cakes with some grilled tempeh and sautéed greens for a savory and satisfying meal, or make mini cakes for an elegant appetizer.

- 1 large yellow onion or 3 shallots, diced small
- 2 carrots, peeled and diced small
- 3 ribs celery, diced small
- 3 cloves garlic, minced
- 1 tablespoon dried thyme
- 1 tablespoon dried basil
- 1 cup long grain brown rice
- ½ cup wild rice
- 7 cups broth, warmed
- ½ cup white wine
- 2 tablespoons finely chopped fresh parsley
- 1 tablespoon vegan margarine
- ¾ cup bread crumbs

Preheat the oven to 350°.
Line a baking sheet with parchment paper and oil the paper.

1. In a heavy saucepan over medium low heat, sauté the onion, carrots, celery and garlic with 2 tablespoons olive oil for approximately 8 minutes until softened.

2. Add the dry herbs and both rices and stir to coat.

3. Add 1 cup warm broth and stir over medium heat until all the liquid is absorbed.

4. Repeat step 3, stirring constantly until all the liquid is absorbed.

5. After the last cup of stock is absorbed, add the ½ cup of white wine and stir until that is absorbed. Stir in the fresh parsley, and then 1 tablespoon vegan margarine.

6. Add ¼ cup of the bread crumbs, and mix well.

7. Spread the risotto out on a plate or baking sheet until cooled.

8. Wet your hands, scoop out ½ cup of mixture at a time and form into balls.

9. Lay the balls down, well spaced, on the oiled parchment lined baking sheet and lightly sprinkle with ½ of the remaining bread crumbs.

10. Lightly flatten the risotto into cakes, then sprinkle the tops with the last of the breadcrumbs.

11. Bake for 15-20 minutes or until golden.

In the meantime, prepare the Leek and Red Pepper Sauce: (recipe follows)

Leek and Red Pepper Sauce

Leek and Red Pepper Sauce
2 medium white onions, diced small
1 tablespoon minced garlic
2 leeks, split in half, thoroughly cleaned, and thinly sliced
2 tablespoons vegan margarine
6 roasted red peppers, thinly sliced
2 tablespoons broth powder
   or 1 vegan bouillon cube, dissolved in ½ cup water
½ teaspoon dried dill
2 teaspoons minced scallion
pinch sea salt
pinch black pepper
1½ teaspoons vegan margarine
minced fresh parsley, for garnish

Leek and Red Pepper Sauce:
1. In a small saucepan over medium heat, sauté onions, garlic, and leeks in margarine until soft.

2. Add the red peppers, broth and dill and sauté for about 2 minutes. Remove from heat.

3. With an immersion blender, pulse until the ingredients combine to create a bright sauce. Stir in the 1½ teaspoons of margarine, and sprinkle liberally with minced parsley
Serve with the risotto cakes.

Drinks, Juices & Smoothies

Juice is a great way to pack a huge punch of raw, organic fruit and vegetable energy into a glass and meet our nutritional needs in our busy lives.

Among the benefits offered by juice are speeding up a sluggish metabolism, cleansing the body and blood of toxic cells, and helping a weak digestive system. Juice also adds chlorophyll to our diet, bringing sunlight's positive properties and energy directly into our circulation, and supplies us with vitamins and minerals we may not be eating daily. With juice you can give your body a break, yet still supply it with easy to absorb fuel.

In this section we give you a jumping off point for an exciting journey into the world of juice. Feel free to experiment withyour own combinations. Cheers!

Bugs Bunny

Serves 1

Freshly juiced carrot with vanilla soy ice cream and crushed ice - sweet! This is a beta-carotene-packed creamsicle in a cup.

1 cup fresh carrot juice (roughly 4 carrots)
3 scoops vanilla soy ice cream
¼ cup crushed ice

1. Pour carrot juice into blender and add scoops of vanilla soy ice cream and ¼ cup crushed ice.
2. Blend until smooth.

At Down to Earth, we prefer Soy Delicious brand soy ice cream.

Circulator

Serves 1

A 2-ounce shot that gets your blood pumping! Liven up a tired body, give a boost to your digestion or zap that nasty cold.

1" piece fresh ginger
½ lemon
cayenne pepper to taste
1 ounce flax seed oil

1. Juice ginger and lemon into a cup.
2. Add the flax oil and approximately ¼ teaspoon cayenne (or to taste) to the cup, and stir.

Fruit Slushie

Serves 1

1 cup apple juice
3 frozen strawberries
2 ounces frozen blueberries
1 frozen banana, cut in small pieces

1. Pour the apple juice into a blender.
2. Add strawberries, blueberries and banana, and blend until smooth.

Chef's Tip:
Prepare for smoothies ahead of time by placing fruit ingredients in bags and freezing. It makes for quicker, thicker, shake-like smoothies.

Good Ol' Carrot

Serves 1

carrots,
about 4 medium for a 12 ounce glass
Optional Additions:
2-3 1½" pieces of beet
1½" piece of fresh ginger
a handful of greens
a small clove of garlic
half an apple

1. Prewash all ingredients you decide to use.

2. Juice any optional ingredients first.

3. Juice the carrots to reach the amount of juice you wish.

Immune Booster

Serves 1

Da Bomb! Tastiest way to get lots of vitamins!

1 small garlic clove
1½" piece of ginger
½ small beet, peeled and cut in pieces
½ lemon
1 handful greens, washed
½ medium apple, washed
    approximately 4 medium carrots, peeled

1. Juice garlic, ginger, beets, then lemon.

2. Juice greens followed by apples.

3. Run enough carrots through the juicer to bring the juice up to 16 ounces.

Live Lemonade

Serves 1

The best lemonade you've ever had - fresh organic lemons and apples with a bit of ginger over ice!

½ lemon
1½" piece fresh ginger
approximately 4 medium apples
4 ounces crushed ice

Optional Additions:
3-4 1½" pieces of peeled fresh beet
a handful of greens, washed

1. Prewash all fruit.
2. Juice lemon, ginger and any optional vegetables first.
3. Juice enough apple to make 12 ounces and add ice.

Maegan's Heartburn Helper

Serves 1

In the old days before pre-packaged medications and 24-hour pharmacies, everybody knew this easy tummy-relief remedy. Now, we proudly pass it down to you. Drink to your health!

2 ounces water
1 teaspoon baking soda

Stir together in a small glass and drink it down. Heartburn's gone!

Rootbeer Float

(photo page 129)

Serves 1

Vanilla ice cream floating in luscious root beer is a dream come true in a glass. This is a fun thing to make with the kids on special occasions. It's a great childhood memory of mine.

3 scoops vanilla soy ice cream
1 12-ounce can all-natural root beer

1. Place the scoops of vanilla soy ice cream in a 16 ounce glass.

2. Slowly and carefully pour the root beer over the ice cream.

Chef's Tip:
Be careful when pouring soda over soy ice cream - the ice cream will rise quickly and can spill over the glass!

Soy Shake

Serves 1

Just like an old fashioned shake without all the dairy. Blend soy milk with your favorite soy ice cream; you can add fruit, nuts, or peanut butter for an extra special treat!

1 cup soymilk
3 scoops soy ice cream

Optional Additions:
strawberries
blueberries
peanut butter
almond butter
bananas

1. Pour soymilk into a blender.

2. Add 3 scoops of the soy ice cream flavor of your choice and any optional additions, and then blend until smooth.

DRINKS, JUICES & SMOOTHIES

Spirulina Rush

Serves 1

This shake is packed with essential fatty acids and spirulina - a food that is a complete protein. Complete proteins supply you with all the essential and non-essential amino acids that help with all body and brain functions. What a rush!

1 cup apple juice
3 ounces blueberries
1 banana, cut in small pieces
2 ounces hemp seeds
1 ounce flax seed oil
1 tablespoon spirulina

1. Pour the apple juice into a blender.
2. Add the fruit, hemp seeds and flax oil, and start blending.
3. With the blender running, slowly add the spirulina, and blend until smooth.

Strawberry Sunrise

Serves 1

Breakfast on the run. On the mornings when you don't have time to prepare a big breakfast, a shake is a great way to start the day. Use our granola in this recipe - it's packed with all kinds of good stuff.

1 cup soymilk, rice milk,
  or apple juice
4 strawberries
1 banana, cut in small pieces
2 ounces Granola (raw, page 117
  or regular, page 167)

1. In a blender, put the 1 cup of liquid of choice.
2. Add fruit and granola and blend until smooth.

Breakfast

We break for breakfast. We have Tofu Scramble on toast frequently at the restaurant to jump start our day as a healthy ritual. In this chapter we share how much fun vegan breakfast can be.

Tiffany's Pancakes are truly scrumptious, especially when served with Tempeh Sausage. Try the Apple Crumb Muffins - a great breakfast when you're on the go. You can use the Granola to add to the trail mix for your little ones. Surprise your mom or dad on Mother's or Father's Day with a fabulous assortment of vegan breakfast dishes accompanied by seasonal fruit. Tempeh Sausage and Gravy Bisquits are a good way to warm up a winter morning, and our Cinnamon Buns are a sweet and decadent dream to wake up to. We hope these favorite breakfast recipes of ours will be yours, too.

Apple Crumb Muffins

Yield: 12 muffins

The apples make these muffins moist and light, and the sweet cinnamon crumb topping makes them decadent, but they contain a fraction of the fat of muffins made with milk and eggs. A delicious combination that is hard to pass up.

Apple Mix
1 tablespoon maple syrup
2 crisp apples (Braeburn or Fuji), peeled, cored and chopped into small cubes
1 tablespoon canola oil
½ teaspoon cinnamon
¼ teaspoon nutmeg

Crumb Topping
1¼ cup unbleached flour
1 cup uncooked rolled oats
½ cup Sucanat
¾ cup solid coconut oil or vegan margarine
½ teaspoon vanilla
1 teaspoon cinnamon
¼ teaspoon nutmeg
pinch sea salt

Dry Ingredients
2 teaspoons baking powder
2 teaspoons baking soda
2 cup unbleached flour
1½ cup whole wheat flour
2 teaspoons cinnamon
1 teaspoon ground ginger

Wet Ingredients
1¼ cups canola oil
1½ cups maple syrup
¼ cup vanilla
1 teaspoon sea salt
2 tablespoons apple cider vinegar
1½ cups water

Preheat the oven to 375°. Lightly oil the tops of muffin tins and insert a dozen cupcake liners. Set aside.

1. In a saucepan, cook the ingredients for the apple mix over medium heat for 4-5 minutes until just slightly softened.

2. Mix together the ingredients for the crumb topping in a bowl, being careful not to over mix, and set aside.

3. In a large mixing bowl, mix all the dry ingredients together.

4. In a third bowl, mix together the wet ingredients.

5. Add the wet ingredients into the dry ingredients and gently mix, just until combined.

6. Gently fold the apple mixture into the batter.

7. Fill the muffin cups halfway full and sprinkle roughly 1 tablespoon of the crumb topping on each.

8. Bake for 18-22 minutes, turning pans halfway through cooking. The muffins are done when a toothpick poked in the middle comes out clean.

These are also delicious with walnuts, ¾ cup either stirred into the batter for extra nuttiness, or mixed into the crumb topping for extra crunch.

Banana Bread

Yield: 1 9" x 5" loaf

This simple banana bread is a great way to use up any extra bananas that may be too ripe to eat. Hemp seeds provide added protein and an omega 3 punch.

2 cups unbleached flour
1½ teaspoons baking powder
½ teaspoon baking soda
½ cup canola oil
¾ cup Sucanat
½ teaspoon sea salt
¼ cup soymilk
¼ cup maple syrup
1 teaspoon vanilla extract
4 large ripe bananas, mashed
½ cup hemp seeds or nuts of choice, roughly chopped

Preheat the oven to 350°.
Lightly oil a loaf pan and set aside.

1. In a large bowl, sift together the flour, baking powder, and baking soda. Set aside.

2. In another bowl, mix together the oil, Sucanat and salt. Stir in the soymilk, maple syrup, and vanilla extract. Add the mashed bananas to the mixture, and mix well.

3. Add the banana mixture and chopped nuts or seeds to the dry ingredients, and mix thoroughly.

4. Pour the batter into the prepared pan and bake 45-50 minutes or until a toothpick comes out clean.

Basic Biscuits

Yield: 12 biscuits

These biscuits are our take on a Southern tradition, and a welcome, easy-to-make addition to a hearty breakfast.

2 cup unbleached flour
2 teaspoons baking powder
½ teaspoon baking soda
½ teaspoon sea salt
6 tablespoons solid coconut oil or vegan margarine
⅔ cup soymilk
1½ teaspoons lemon juice

Preheat the oven to 350°. Line a baking sheet with parchment paper.

1. Sift the dry ingredients together into a mixing bowl.

2. Cut the margarine or solid coconut oil into the flour mixture until it resembles a coarse meal.

3. Make a well in the center of the mixture and pour in the soymilk and lemon juice.

4. Mix together until just moistened, then roll out to ½" thickness.

5. Cut into 2" circles and place the circles on the prepared baking sheet. Re-roll the scraps and make up the rest of the dough into biscuits.

6. Bake for 8-12 minutes or until golden brown.

Tempeh Sausage and Gravy Biscuits

Serves 8

This tasty combo is filled with savory flavors of sage and fennel. The sausage is versatile and easy to prepare and can be made into patties or crumbled. Try it as a delicious topping for pizza. The country gravy is great on mashed potatoes or as a variation to brown gravy, or add it to a soup with seitan and create a hearty country stew.

8 Basic Biscuits (facing page)

Tempeh Sausage
8 ounces Marinated Tempeh (page 28)
1½ cloves garlic, minced
1 tablespoon canola oil
2 tablespoons tamari
⅓ teaspoon dried marjoram
pinch ground sage
½ teaspoon dried thyme
½ teaspoon paprika
⅛ teaspoon cayenne
¾ teaspoon fennel seeds
black pepper, to taste
¼ cup unbleached flour
cornmeal, for dredging
oil, for coating parchment

Herb Gravy
¼ cup nutritional yeast
½ cup whole wheat flour
2 cups water
2 tablespoons tamari
2 tablespoons extra virgin olive oil
½ teaspoon black pepper

Preheat the oven to 400°.
Line a baking sheet with parchment paper and brush liberally with oil.

Make the Tempeh Sausage:
1. Cut the tempeh in half and grate it finely, using a box grater.

2. Add garlic, 1 tablespoon oil, tamari, the herbs and spices, and flour. Mix together, then form into 3½" patties and dredge in cornmeal.

3. Place the patties on the prepared baking sheet, and bake for 15 minutes or until crisped on the outside.

Make the Herb Gravy:

1. Put the nutritional yeast and flour in a 1-quart saucepan and toast over medium heat until light brown.

2. Turn the heat down to very low, and slowly whisk in the oil to form a roux.

3. Gradually whisk in the water and tamari until the gravy is smooth.

4. Raise the heat back to medium and continue cooking, stirring constantly with the whisk until thickened.

Serve a tempeh patty on a biscuit and top it with the herb gravy.

Cinnamon Buns

Yield: 12-16 rolls

Hot, sticky, sweet cinnamon-infused buns… who can resist them? Add raisins or chopped nuts for another variation. Enjoy these scrumptious cinnamon buns with a cup of coffee or tea for a nearly guilt-free breakfast treat.

Buns
- 3 tablespoons yeast
- ¾ cup Sucanat or brown sugar
- 3 cups soymilk
- ½ cup coconut oil or vegan margarine, melted, at room temperature
- 5½ cups spelt flour
- 2 teaspoons sea salt
- ½ cup unbleached flour, if needed
- 1 heaping tablespoon cinnamon
- 1 cup Sucanat or brown sugar
- ½ cup maple syrup

Glaze
- 1½ cups powdered Florida Crystals or powdered sugar
- 1½ teaspoons vanilla extract
- 1½ tablespoons water
- ½ teaspoon cinnamon

Preheat the oven to 375°. Line one large or two small baking sheets with parchment and set aside.

1. Mix the yeast and Sucanat or brown sugar in a large mixing bowl.
2. Warm soymilk over medium heat for 1-2 minutes (until it reaches about 104° on an instant-read thermometer), then add to Sucanat-yeast mixture and let sit in a warm place for 10 minutes.
3. Stir in the coconut oil or melted margarine, add 1 cup spelt flour, and mix well.
4. Sprinkle in the salt, then continue gradually adding flour and mixing until you have an elastic dough that is soft but not sticky.
5. Knead the dough for 3-5 minutes until it bounces back when pressed lightly with a finger.
6. Transfer the dough to an oiled bowl and let it rest, covered, for 15 minutes or longer until the dough doubles in size.
7. Punch down and knead the dough for a minute or two.
8. Roll the dough out to a ¼" thick rectangle.
9. Mix together the cinnamon and 1½ cups Sucanat or brown sugar and sprinkle over the dough with a bit more on the quarter nearest you.
10. Drizzle the maple syrup across the surface of the dough.
11. Roll the dough evenly from the bottom away from you to create a long tube.
12. Cut the tube into 12 or more large rolls.
13. Place the rolls evenly approximately 2-3" apart, press down, and let sit for 10 minutes.
14. Bake the rolls until golden, about 10 minutes. Turn pan around and bake for an additional minute.
15. While the rolls are baking, blend the Florida Crystals, if using, in a blender or spice grinder until powdered.
16. Mix the powdered sugar or Florida Crystals with the vanilla, water and cinnamon, and set aside.
17. Remove the rolls from the oven, and spread the glaze over the buns while still hot.

French Toast

Serves 4   Yield: 8 slices

This is a simple way to create a fun breakfast. Use a thick slice of French baguette to soak up the delicious coating, and serve with fresh fruit, a sprinkle of cinnamon, and maple syrup.

2 cups Almond Milk (page 25)
¼ cup unbleached flour
2 tablespoons canola oil
2 tablespoons nutritional yeast
½ teaspoon sea salt
6 tablespoons maple syrup
1½ teaspoons cinnamon
8 slices French baguette
  or whole grain bread
2 tablespoons canola oil
maple syrup, for serving
Fruit Sauce, for serving (page 185)

1. Whisk together the Almond Milk, flour, 2 tablespoons oil, yeast, salt, maple syrup and cinnamon in a medium mixing bowl.

2. Dip the bread slices into the mixture on both sides until saturated.

3. Heat the remaining 2 tablespoons oil on a griddle or in a skillet and cook the slices until golden on each side.

4. Serve hot with maple syrup or fruit sauce.

Adam's Ginger Oat Waffles with Chamomile Pine Nut Cream & Nectarines

Serves 6

Wheat-free. Top with whichever in-season fresh fruits suit your fancy. Peaches in the summer and juicy pears in the fall and winter are especially nice.

Cream
1½ cups water
½ cup chamomile flowers, fresh or dried
2 cloves
1 green cardamom pod
¾ cup pine nuts, lightly toasted
½ cup Sucanat
pinch sea salt

Waffles
1½ cups uncooked rolled oats
½ cup pine nuts, lightly toasted
2¼ cups water
1 tablespoon extra virgin olive oil
1 tablespoon ground ginger
½ teaspoon ground cardamom
pinch sea salt
⅓ cup Sucanat

2 nectarines, sliced thin

1. Bring the water for the cream to a boil in a small saucepan.

2. Remove from the heat and add the chamomile, cloves and cardamom.

3. Let steep, covered, for 10 minutes.

4. Meanwhile, place the remaining cream ingredients into a blender. Strain the chamomile infusion into the blender.

5. Blend at high speed until the cream is smooth.

6. Chill the cream in the freezer while you make the waffles.

7. Pre-heat the waffle iron.

8. Meanwhile, place the oats and the pine nuts in a blender and blend at medium speed while gradually adding the water.

9. When the mixture is smooth, add the remaining batter ingredients.

10. Pour the batter onto a lightly oiled or non-stick waffle iron, and cook until golden brown and cooked through.

Serve waffles drizzled with generous spoonfuls of cream, and top with nectarine or other fruit slices and a pinch of cinnamon.

Granola

Yield: 8 cups

Store-bought cereals are expensive and often not nutritious. Clusters of oats, nuts, and seeds make this granola rich in calcium, protein and minerals, and it's very easy to make. Enjoy it with your favorite beverage, sprinkle it over yogurt, or add to a smoothie. Kids will love it as a snack, too.

Dry Ingredients
6 cups uncooked rolled oats
1 cup chopped pecans
1 cup pumpkin seeds, chopped in large pieces with a knife
1 cup sunflower seeds
¾ cup hemp seeds
2 teaspoons cinnamon
¼ teaspoon nutmeg

Wet Ingredients
1 cup canola oil
¾ cup maple syrup
½ cup rice syrup
2 teaspoons vanilla extract
¼ teaspoon sea salt

Preheat the oven to 350°.
Line two large baking sheets with parchment paper.

1. In a large mixing bowl, mix the dry ingredients.

2. In a separate mixing bowl, mix the wet ingredients until well combined.

3. Add together the wet ingredients to the dry and mix well.

4. Spread the mixture out on the prepared baking sheets, and bake for 6 minutes.

5. Remove from the oven, stir well, and return to the oven, baking an additional 6 minutes.

6. Remove from the oven and let cool 20 minutes.

Will keep stored in an airtight container for several weeks.

Lemon Blueberry Scones

Yield: 12 scones

These scones are just sweet enough and loaded with blueberries, a great antioxidant-rich food. Make these and you will definitely want to invite friends over for a tea party.

3 cups unbleached flour
1 teaspoon salt
1 tablespoon baking powder
½ teaspoon baking soda
½ cup chopped walnuts
2 cups blueberries
¾ cup canola or other flavorless oil
1 lemon, zested and juiced
¼ cup Florida Crystals, + 2 tablespoons for sprinkling on top
¼ cup maple syrup
¾ cup vanilla soymilk
1½ teaspoons apple cider vinegar
1 tablespoon vanilla extract
1½ teaspoons lemon extract

Preheat oven to 375°.
Line 2 baking sheets with parchment paper.

1. In a large bowl, whisk together the flour, salt, baking powder, baking soda, walnuts, and blueberries.

2. In a separate bowl, whisk together the oil, lemon juice, lemon zest, Florida Crystals, maple syrup, soymilk, vinegar, vanilla, and lemon extract and mix well.

3. Using a rubber spatula, fold the wet mixture into the dry mixture until just combined. Don't overmix.

4. Drop the dough in ¼ cup scoops 2" apart onto the baking sheets.

5. Bake for 20 minutes or until a toothpick inserted into the center of a scone comes out clean.

Michelle's Blueberry Sour Cream Coffee Cake

Serves 8   Yield: 1 9" cake

Michelle has been a part of the Down to Earth family since nearly the beginning. She loves to bake vegan treats and has generously shared this scrumptious coffee cake, which is as special as she is. Using tofu sour cream to give it its moist texture and juicy blueberries, this cake will be devoured quickly.

Topping
1 cup whole wheat flour
½ cup Florida Crystals
½ cup vegan margarine, chilled

Cake
¾ cup vegan margarine
1 cup Florida Crystals
¼ cup unsweetened apple sauce
1½ teaspoons vanilla extract
2 cups unbleached flour
1 teaspoon baking powder
1 cup store-bought tofu sour cream
1 cup fresh blueberries

Preheat the oven to 350°.
Grease a 9" cake pan and set aside.

1. For the topping, mix together the whole wheat flour and Florida Crystals.

2. Cut in the ½ cup vegan margarine until crumbly, and refrigerate until ready to use.

3. In a medium mixing bowl, cream together the ¾ cup vegan margarine and 1 cup Florida Crystals.

4. Mix in the apple sauce and vanilla.

5. Into a large mixing bowl, sift the flour and baking powder.

6. Add the wet mixture and the tofu sour cream to the dry mixture and fold together with a rubber spatula until just mixed.

7. Gently fold in the blueberries.

8. Spread into greased cake pan and crumble the topping evenly over the batter.

9. Bake for 30 minutes, or until a toothpick inserted in the center of the cake comes out clean.

Papaya Delight

Serves 2

An easy-to-prepare delight, loaded with simple goodness - enzymes, protein and live cultures. Topped with our granola, it makes a complete and satisfying breakfast.

1 ripe papaya
8 ounces plain or vanilla soy yogurt (we love Whole Soy brand)
½ cup Granola (raw, page 117 or regular, page 167)

1. Slice the papaya in half lengthwise and gently scoop out the seeds with a teaspoon.

2. Fill each hollow with yogurt and top with granola

Chef's Tip:
Cut a small slice off the underside of the papaya halves to help them lie flat.

Quiche

Serves 8   Yield: 1 9" quiche

This is an appetizing and zesty egg-free version of a Sunday brunch favorite - light and flaky crust filled with a blend of herbed tofu and spices. Vary the vegetables with the seasons for a change of flavor. This can be cut into smaller bites for a great party food.

Coconut Oil Crust
1½ cups unbleached flour
½ teaspoon sea salt
1 tablespoon Florida Crystals
¼ teaspoon baking powder
6 tablespoons coconut oil, chilled
¼ cup ice water, or as needed

Quiche Filling
1 14-ounce block firm tofu
½ cup nutritional yeast
1 tablespoon tamari
1½ teaspoons white miso
½ teaspoon thyme
½ teaspoon basil
1 teaspoon sea salt
½ teaspoon black pepper
⅛ teaspoon turmeric
½ teaspoon dry mustard
2 tablespoons extra virgin olive oil
½ large onion, diced
3 cloves garlic, chopped
½ medium zucchini, diced small
½ medium carrot, shredded
½ cup broccoli florets, blanched

Preheat the oven to 400°.

1. Sift together the flour, salt, Florida Crystals, and baking powder.

2. Using a fork or pastry cutter, cut the coconut oil into the flour to form a coarse meal.

3. Add the water slowly until the dough comes together.

4. Roll the dough out and fit into a 9" pie plate or tart pan and lay parchment over the crust.

5. Weigh down the bottom of the pie crust with dried beans or uncooked rice, and bake for 10-12 minutes until golden. Remove from the oven, remove the beans or rice, peel off the parchment and set aside to cool.

6. Turn the oven down to 350°.

7. Crumble the tofu into the bowl of a food processor and process until smooth. Add the nutritional yeast, tamari, miso, thyme, basil, salt, pepper, turmeric and dry mustard and blend well.
Transfer to a medium sized bowl and set aside.

8. In a sauté pan, heat the oil, then add the onion and garlic, and sauté until soft.

9. Add the zucchini, carrot, and broccoli, and sauté, stirring until soft.

10. Add the sautéed vegetables to the tofu mixture and stir until combined.

11. Pour the filling into the prebaked crust and bake for 20-25 minutes until golden brown.

This quiche may be served hot or at room temperature.

Tempeh Bacun

Yield: 20 slices

A crisp, smoky temptation. The thinner you slice the tempeh and the longer you cook it, the crispier and crunchier it will be. A great breakfast treat, this recipe has many other uses from sandwiches to salads; it stores well and is good to have around.

3 tablespoons olive oil
2 tablespoons maple syrup
1½ teaspoons tamari
¾ teaspoon liquid smoke
8 ounces tempeh, sliced ⅛" thick

Preheat the oven to 350°.
Line a baking sheet with parchment paper.

1. Mix all the liquid ingredients together. Brush the surface of the baking sheet with some of the mixture, then lay the tempeh slices on the sheet. Brush tempeh slices with the remaining liquid.

2. Bake for 8-10 minutes.

Tiffany's Pancakes

(photo page 127)

Yield: 16 large pancakes

A true classic stands the test of time and so does Tiffany. A long-time kitchen mate, she shares her love of pancakes with us. These moist and hefty pancakes will make you want to be the first person up to surprise the ones you love with these treats.

2 cups unbleached flour
½ teaspoon sea salt
1½ teaspoons baking powder
½ teaspoon baking soda
½ cup water
¼ cup canola oil, + extra for oiling pan
1½ cup vanilla soymilk
1 teaspoon apple cider vinegar
1 teaspoon vanilla

¾ cup chopped fruit or nuts
vegan margarine
safflower oil for griddle
maple syrup for serving

1. Into a large bowl, sift the flour, salt, baking soda and baking powder.

2. In a medium bowl, combine the water, oil, soymilk, vinegar and vanilla, and whisk until thoroughly combined.

3. Add the liquid ingredients to the dry ingredients, and whisk until all lumps are gone.

4. Using a rubber spatula, fold in the fruit or nuts.

5. Oil a griddle and heat over medium heat.

6. Pour ⅓ cup of batter onto the heated griddle and fry until the underside is golden brown.

7. Flip pancake with spatula and fry until the second side is golden. Keep pancakes warm on a foil-covered plate in a 250° oven until ready to serve.

8. Serve hot with vegan margarine and maple syrup.

Chef's Tip:
For extra fluffy pancakes, replace the water with ½ cup of seltzer water.

Tofu Scramble

Serves 4

The union of tofu and vegetables makes for a tasty breakfast. Create new flavor combinations by adding different seasonal vegetables and spices. The nutritional yeast gives this recipe a rich flavor, and the turmeric adds bright yellow color.

1 14-ounce block firm tofu
3 tablespoons extra virgin olive oil
1 medium onion, diced
3 cloves garlic, minced
1 medium red bell pepper, seeded and diced
¾ cup shredded carrot
1 cup diced zucchini
3 tablespoons tamari
¼ cup nutritional yeast
1 teaspoon sea salt
¼ teaspoon Spike
½ teaspoon turmeric
¼ teaspoon paprika

1. Press the tofu according to the instructions on page 94, see Chef's Tip.

2. In a medium sauté pan, heat the oil, and sauté the onions and garlic until soft.

3. Crumble the tofu into the pan with the onions and garlic, and sauté for a minute.

4. Add the remaining ingredients and sauté until the tofu gets slightly brown.

You can also punch up the flavor and nutrition by adding ½ cup of chopped spinach toward the end of cooking.

Desserts

Sweets are among our favorite things. Customers and friends have been clamoring for many of these classic recipes, which we have kept secret until now!

We look forward to celebrations as an occasion for some new cake or other fabulous dessert treat. We serve fun vegan desserts everyday at the restaurant, including our decadent Chocolate Ganache Cake. Around the holidays, we always make our Pumpkin Cheesecake; it's so popular we could serve it year round.

Cookies are also an important part of our lives. We make many varieties, and the possibilities are endless. Our most popular one is the Magic Cookie, a crunchy, nutty, chewy confection that could almost be a meal! We also make lots of delicious wheat-free cookies and encourage baking with alternatives.

We dispel the myth that vegan baked goods lack sweetness, fantastic texture and variety. We do use natural, alternative sweeteners but we have to admit - sugar in any form is sweet! We try to make it a little less harmful for you and the earth by using organic and more sustainable preparations of cane sugar, the way it's been used for centuries. All of our recipes are 100% animal free, using egg-free leaveners and healthier fats to produce equal or better results than what is used in conventional baking. We pride ourselves on the unanimous great reviews we get from people new to vegan baked goods - they love our desserts every time!!

Hempseed Cookies

Yield: 16 cookies

Not just chocolate chip. These crispy cookies are made from spelt flour and have the added bonus of hemp seeds to make them healthy, as well as delicious.

1½ cups spelt flour
½ teaspoons baking powder
1½ teaspoons egg replacer
2 tablespoons water
½ cup Sucanat
1 cup Florida Crystals
¼ cup coconut oil, solid
2 teaspoons vanilla extract
½ teaspoon salt
¾ cup chocolate chips
¼ cup hemp seeds
¼ cup water

1. Combine flour and baking powder in a large bowl.

2. In a separate bowl, mix together egg replacer and 2 tablespoons water.

3. Add the Sucanat, Florida Crystals and coconut oil to the egg replacer, and cream well by hand or with an electric mixer.

4. Add the vanilla and salt to the creamed mixture.

5. Mix the wet ingredients into the dry ingredients.

6. Stir in the chocolate chips and hemp seeds.

7. Add the remaining water slowly, and then let the batter chill for 20 minutes in the fridge.

8. Meanwhile, preheat the oven to 350°. Line a large baking sheet with parchment paper.

9. Scoop the batter into golf ball sized balls. Space 2" apart on the baking sheet, flatten with your palm and bake approximately 18 minutes, until golden brown.

10. Remove from oven and let cool on the baking sheet.

Jam Dot Cookies
(Peanut Butter and Jam Cookies)

Yield: 14 large cookies

Dry Ingredients
2½ cups roasted salted peanuts
2½ cups uncooked rolled oats
2½ cups spelt flour
pinch sea salt
1½ teaspoons cinnamon

Wet Ingredients
1¼ cups maple syrup
1¼ cups canola oil

raspberry fruit spread, for filling

Preheat the oven to 350°.
Line a large baking sheet with parchment paper and set aside.

1. Pulse the peanuts in a food processor or blender to a medium grind. Transfer to a medium bowl and set aside.

2. Repeat the process for the oats, pulsing until finely ground, and add to the bowl with the ground peanuts.

3. Add the flour, salt and cinnamon, and stir to combine.

4. In a medium sized bowl, combine the wet ingredients.

5. Add the wet ingredients to the dry ingredients and mix until combined.

6. Scoop ¼ cups of dough onto the baking sheet. Space 2" apart and flatten with your palm.

7. Indent the middle of each cookie and fill with about 1 tablespoon fruit spread.

8. Bake 15 - 20 minutes until golden.

9. Remove from oven and let cool on the baking sheet.

Chef's Tip:
A deeper well ensures that the jam does not bubble over during baking.

Magic Cookies

(photo page 129)

Yield: 9 large cookies

These cookies - a combination of coconut, carrots, pecans, and chocolate chips baked until golden brown - make magic happen. The only near riot that ever occurred in Red Bank is said to have happened when we ran out of these cookies.

Dry Ingredients
1 cup unbleached flour
¾ cup shredded carrot
1 cup coconut
1 cup Florida Crystals
1 cup uncooked rolled oats
½ teaspoon baking powder
¼ teaspoon salt

Wet Ingredients
2 tablespoons solid coconut oil, melted
⅓ cup water
¼ cup canola oil
1½ teaspoons vanilla extract
⅔ cup chocolate chips
2 cups pecans, chopped

Preheat the oven to 350°.
Line a large baking sheet with parchment paper and set aside.

1. In a large bowl, mix together the flour, carrots, coconut, Florida Crystals, oats, baking powder and salt.

2. In a separate bowl, mix together the coconut oil, water, canola oil, and vanilla.

3. Add the wet ingredients to the dry ingredients, and mix well to combine.

4. Stir in the chocolate chips and pecans.

5. Use a ¼ cup scoop to place mounds of dough onto the prepared baking sheet. Space 2" apart and flatten with your palm. Bake 10-15 minutes, until golden brown.

6. Remove from oven and let cool on the baking sheet.

Maple Pecan Cookies

Yield: 12 large cookies

A delicious treat with tea or coffee, we also use this basic cookie for our cheesecake crust. It contains no refined sugar.

Wet Ingredients
1 cup canola oil
1 cup maple syrup
2 tablespoons vanilla extract
¼ teaspoon salt

Dry Ingredients
3 cups pecans, toasted
2 cups oats
2 cups spelt flour

pecan halves, for garnish

Preheat the oven to 350°.
Line a large baking sheet with parchment paper and set aside.

1. In a medium-sized bowl, combine the oil, maple syrup, vanilla, and salt.

2. Pulse the pecans in a food processor or blender to a medium grind. Transfer to a medium bowl and set aside.

3. Repeat the process for the oats, pulsing until finely ground, and add them to the bowl with the ground pecans.

4. Add the spelt flour to the pecans and oat flour, and mix to combine.

5. Add the wet ingredients to the dry, and mix thoroughly.

6. Scoop out ¼ cup measurements of dough onto the prepared baking sheet. Space 2" apart and flatten with your palm.

7. Bake for 20 minutes until golden.

8. Remove from oven and let cool on the baking sheet.

Oatmeal Raisin Cookies

Yield: 12 large cookies

These cookies are an old-fashioned standby, but never fail to bring joy and smiles to the mouths of those who eat them.

3 teaspoons egg replacer
¼ cup water
1 cup coconut oil
1½ cups Florida Crystals
1½ cups Sucanat
2 teaspoons vanilla extract
6 tablespoons soymilk
1 cup canola oil
1 cup water
4½ cups unbleached flour
1 teaspoon baking powder
1 teaspoon salt
2½ cups rolled oats
2 teaspoons cinnamon
1 teaspoon nutmeg
¼ teaspoon ground ginger
1 cup raisins
½ cup chopped walnuts

Preheat the oven to 350°.
Line a large baking sheet with parchment paper and set aside.

1. Mix together the egg replacer and ¼ cup water.

2. Add the coconut oil, Florida Crystals and Sucanat, and cream together.

3. Add the vanilla, soymilk, oil and remaining water, and mix well.

4. In a separate bowl, mix together the flour, baking powder, salt, oats, cinnamon, nutmeg and ginger.

5. Add the dry ingredients to the wet ingredients, and mix well.

6. Stir in the raisins and walnuts.

7. Scoop into ¼ cup mounds onto the baking sheet. Space 2" apart and flatten with your palm. Bake 15-18 minutes.

8. Remove from oven and let cool on the baking sheet.

Sugar Cookies

Yield: 12 large cookies

These crisp cookies are easy and fabulous to make around the holidays. If chilled, they can be rolled out, cut, and decorated like traditional butter sugar cookies

Dry Ingredients
4½ cups spelt flour
¾ teaspoon baking soda
½ teaspoon salt
½ teaspoon cinnamon

Wet Ingredients
3 tablespoons egg replacer
¾ cup water
2¼ cups Florida Crystals
1 tablespoon vanilla extract
1 cup + 2 tablespoons flavorless oil
2 tablespoons maple syrup

Variation:
Ginger Spice Cookies
-replace maple syrup with molasses
-add 2 teaspoons ginger powder
-add 1 teaspoon cinnamon
-add ½ teaspoon nutmeg
-add 1 teaspoon allspice

Preheat the oven to 350°.
Line a large baking sheet with parchment paper and set aside.

1. Sift the flour, baking soda, salt and cinnamon together into a large bowl.

2. In a separate bowl, mix the egg replacer and the water, then mix in the Florida Crystals, vanilla, oil and maple syrup.

3. Pour the wet ingredients into the dry ingredients, and mix together thoroughly.

4. Roll into ¼ cup balls, place on the prepared baking sheet, space 2" apart and flatten with your palm.

5. Bake 15-18 minutes or until golden.

6. Remove from oven and let cool on the baking sheet.

Blondies

Yield: 9 blondies

Coffee flavor, chocolate and a nutty butterscotch taste make these decadent blondies a winner with everyone. For a caffeine free treat, leave out the coffee, or use decaffeinated coffee.

Dry Ingredients
1 cup whole wheat flour
1 cup + 6 tablespoons unbleached flour
1 teaspoon baking powder
1 teaspoon salt

Wet Ingredients
½ cup Sucanat
½ cup grain coffee powder
1 cup canola oil
1 cup maple syrup
½ cup soymilk
¼ cup vanilla extract

2 tablespoons tahini
1 tablespoon peanut butter
1 cup chocolate chips

Preheat the oven to 350°.
Lay a sheet of parchment on the bottom of an 8"x8" pan.

1. Sift the dry ingredients together into a large mixing bowl.

2. In a separate bowl, mix together the Sucanat, coffee powder, oil, maple syrup, soymilk and vanilla.

3. Add the wet ingredients to the dry ingredients and mix until moistened.

4. Stir in the tahini and peanut butter, then stir in the chocolate chips.

5. Spread the batter into the prepared baking pan and bake for 18 minutes, or until a toothpick inserted into the center comes out clean.

6. Remove from the oven and let cool on a rack to room temperature. Cut into 9 equal squares.

Brownies

Yield: 12-15 brownies

Super rich chocolaty goodness, these brownies beg to be eaten with a tall glass of your favorite soy or nut milk. Spread chocolate ganache on top of these to drive your friends and family into a chocoholic frenzy.

Wet Ingredients
3 tablespoons egg replacer
¾ cup water
1½ cups soymilk
1¼ cups oil
1 tablespoon vanilla extract
3 cups Sucanat

Dry Ingredients
2¼ cups cocoa
2 cups unbleached flour
¾ teaspoon baking powder
¾ teaspoon salt
1½ cups chopped nuts

Preheat the oven to 350°.
Grease a 9"x13" pan, line with parchment paper, and set aside.

1. Whisk together the egg replacer and water and then mix with the rest of the wet ingredients and Sucanat.

2. In a separate bowl, mix together the cocoa, flour, baking powder, salt and nuts.

3. Add the wet ingredients to the dry ingredients and mix together.

4. Pour into the prepared pan and bake for 25-30 minutes or until a toothpick inserted into the center comes out clean.

5. Cool on a rack to room temperature. When cool, cut into squares.

Cheesecake

Serves 8   Yield: 1 9" cake

This tofu cheesecake is wheat-free, cholesterol free and as creamy and delicious as what your Mom used to make.

Crust:
Dry Ingredients
1 cup uncooked rolled oats
1 cup spelt flour
1½ cups pecans, toasted

Wet Ingredients
½ cup canola oil
½ cup maple syrup
1 tablespoon vanilla extract
⅛ teaspoon sea salt

Filling
2 14-ounce blocks extra-firm tofu
½ cup canola oil
½ teaspoon sea salt
¼ cup lemon juice
1 cup Florida Crystals
1 tablespoon vanilla extract

Preheat the oven to 350°.
Grease a 9" springform pan and set aside.

1. Grind oats and cooled pecans in a food processor until fine.

2. Combine oats, pecans and flour in a mixing bowl.

3. In a separate bowl, combine the oil, maple syrup, vanilla and salt.

4. Mix wet ingredients into the dry ingredients and press into the prepared pan. Bake for 10 minutes, then remove from the oven and set aside.

5. Combine the ingredients for the filling in a blender or food processor, and blend until smooth.

6. Pour the filling into the pan with the crust and bake for 20 minutes.

7. Remove from the oven and let cool to room temperature. Refrigerate for 1 hour before serving.

Serve with Fruit Sauce (recipe follows).

Fruit Sauce

Yield: 2 cups

This sauce is sweet and delicious. Try it over ice cream or with our cheesecake or chocolate ganache cake.

3 cups fresh or frozen fruit of choice
3 tablespoons lemon juice
½ cup Florida Crystals
¼ cup arrowroot powder
¼ cup cold water
pinch of sea salt

1. In a small saucepan combine the fruit, lemon juice, and Florida Crystals and cook over medium low heat for 3-4 minutes, stirring until the sugar dissolves.

2. Dissolve the arrowroot in cold water, making sure to combine so that it makes a cloudy liquid with no settling powder on the bottom.

3. Add the arrowroot mixture to the fruit in the pot, stirring continuously to avoid lumps. Add a pinch of salt and let the mixture cook together for 3-5 minutes until it has thickened.

4. Let the sauce cool. Store in the refrigerator for up to 3 days.

For a thinner sauce, remove the sauce from heat before adding the arrowroot, add a pinch of salt, let cool and blend. Pour the mixture through a sieve, and you will have a smooth and refined sauce.

Pumpkin Cheesecake

Serves 8   Yield: 1 9" cake

Pumpkin cheesecake is a holiday classic flavored with the sweet spices of autumn - cinnamon, nutmeg and ginger. The pecan crust adds the final touch to make this pie part of your family's holiday tradition.

Pecan Cookie Crust

Dry Ingredients
1 cup uncooked rolled oats, finely ground
1 cup whole wheat pastry flour
1½ cups pecans, toasted and ground

Wet Ingredients
½ cup safflower oil
½ cup maple syrup
1 tablespoon vanilla extract
⅛ teaspoon sea salt

Pumpkin Filling

1½ cups pumpkin purée or
    1-15 ounce can pumpkin purée
1½ 14-ounce blocks extra-firm tofu
¼ cup safflower oil
¾ teaspoon salt
¼ cup maple syrup
1 cup Sucanat
1 tablespoon vanilla extract
¾ teaspoon cinnamon
¼ teaspoon nutmeg
½ teaspoon ground ginger

Preheat the oven to 350°.

For the Crust:
1. Combine the oats, flour and pecans in a mixing bowl.

2. In a separate bowl, combine the wet ingredients for the crust.

3. Mix the wet ingredients into the dry and press into a 9" springform pan to form a crust.

For the filling:

1. Combine all of the filling ingredients in a blender or food processor, and process until smooth, pausing to scrape down the sides of the container with a spatula as you go.

2. Pour the filling into the prepared crust.

3. Bake 25 minutes.

4. Remove from the oven and cool on a rack to room temperature. Cover and chill for 4 hours before serving.

Chocolate Cake

Serves 8   **Yield: 2 9" layers**

These basic chocolate layers are the starting point for many of the cakes that follow.

Dry Ingredients
2 cups unbleached flour
½ cup cocoa
½ cup Sucanat
2 teaspoons baking powder
2 teaspoons baking soda
1 teaspoon salt

Wet Ingredients
½ cup canola oil
1 cup vanilla soymilk
½ cup water
1 cup maple syrup
1 tablespoon chocolate extract
2 teaspoons apple cider vinegar

Preheat the oven to 350°.
Oil two 9" round cake pans and set aside.

1. Sift the flour, cocoa, Sucanat, baking powder, baking soda and salt into a large bowl and mix together.

2. In a separate bowl, mix together the oil, soymilk, water, maple syrup, chocolate extract and vinegar.

3. Pour the wet ingredients into the dry ingredients and mix until incorporated.

4. Divide the batter evenly between the two prepared pans, and bake for 18-22 minutes, until a toothpick inserted into the center of the cake comes out clean.

5. Cool the layers on racks for 10 minutes, and remove from pans. Cool to room temperature before frosting.

Chocolate Ganache Cake

Serves 8   Yield: 1 9" cake

On the menu nearly every week since we opened our doors, this decadent chocolate fantasy put us on the map for top-notch vegan desserts. We now gladly pass it on to you enjoy!

2 9" Chocolate Cakes, cooled (page 187)

Chocolate Ganache
Yield: 1 pint
2 cups chocolate chips
1 cup vanilla soymilk

1. Put the chocolate chips in a medium heatproof bowl.
2. Slowly heat the soymilk to boiling.
3. Pour the boiling milk over the chips and let sit for 1-2 minutes, until the chocolate is softened.
4. Whisk the chips and milk together for about 2 minutes, incorporating to a velvety gloss.
5. Refrigerate the ganache for at least 1½ hours until solidified.
6. Frost the cake and serve.

Serve drizzled with Chocolate Sauce (see below) for a chocoholic delight.

Chocolate Sauce

Yield: 1 pint

This recipe makes a thin, rich chocolate sauce that is a fitting accompaniment to many desserts.

1 cup chocolate chips
2 cups vanilla soymilk

Follow the directions above for Chocolate Ganache through step 4.

Try this drizzled over cakes or ice cream – anywhere a festive finish is desired.

German Chocolate Cake (photo page 130)

Serves 8   Yield: 1 9" cake

The toasted pecans and coconut in this topping for our basic chocolate cake take it to another level of indulgence.

2 9" Chocolate Cakes, cooled (page 187)

Coconut Frosting
¼ cup egg replacer
1 cup water
⅔ cup coconut milk
⅓ cup Sucanat
¼ cup coconut oil
1½ cups toasted coconut
1¼ cups chopped pecans
1 teaspoon coconut extract
pinch nutmeg
½ teaspoon vanilla extract
1 teaspoon sea salt

1. In a 2 quart bowl, whisk together the egg replacer, water, coconut milk and Sucanat.

2. Cook mixture over medium low heat for 3 minutes.

3. Add the coconut oil, toasted coconut, pecans, coconut extract, and nutmeg, stirring constantly until the mixture has thickened slightly.

4. Add the vanilla and continue to cook for about 2 minutes.

5. Add the salt and cook until the mixture has darkened to an even shade of tan.

6. Refrigerate the frosting until set, then frost the cake.

Peanut Butter Chocolate Cake

Serves 8   Yield: 1 9" cake

The winning combination of chocolate and peanut butter can't go wrong. Our rich chocolate cake with this luscious whipped peanut butter frosting is a case in point.

2 9" Chocolate Cakes, cooled (page 187)

Peanut Butter Frosting
1 cup natural peanut butter
7 ounces coconut milk
½ cup coconut oil, solid
½ cup maple syrup
2 teaspoons sea salt
2 cups Sucanat
2 14-ounce blocks firm tofu
1½ tablespoons vanilla extract

1. Combine the peanut butter, coconut milk, coconut oil, maple syrup, sea salt and Sucanat in a blender, and blend until combined.

2. Crumble the tofu blocks into the blender, add the vanilla and blend on high speed, pausing occasionally to scraping down the sides to ensure even mixing.

3. Frost the cake and serve.

Drizzle the plates with Chocolate Sauce (page 188) for a dazzling finish!

Vanilla Cake

Yield: 2 9" layers

This is a basic vanilla cake recipe that can be a great jumping off point. Try it with vanilla frosting or chocolate ganache, or use your imagination and have fun with this delicious base.

Dry Ingredients
3½ cups unbleached flour
2 teaspoons baking powder
2 teaspoons baking soda
1 teaspoon salt

Wet Ingredients
⅔ cup canola oil
1½ cups maple syrup
1⅓ cups water
¼ cup vanilla extract
⅛ cup apple cider vinegar

Preheat the oven to 350°.
Oil two 9" round pans and line with parchment paper.

1. Into a large bowl, sift together the flour, baking powder, baking soda and salt.

2. In a medium sized bowl, combine the oil, maple syrup, water, vanilla, and vinegar.

3. Pour the wet ingredients into the dry and mix until combined.

4. Divide the batter evenly between the prepared pans.

5. Bake for approximately 20 minutes, until the tops are golden and a toothpick inserted into the center comes out clean.

6. Cool the layers on a rack for 10 minutes and remove from pans. Let cool to room temperature before frosting.

Chef's Tip:
Using both oil and parchment paper to line the cake pans ensures that the cake releases cleanly from the bottom of the pan. When the layers are cool, run a thin knife around the outside edge of the cake pan and invert the layers onto a plate or baking rack. Then peel the parchment paper up from the cake. Voila! Clean finish every time.

Vanilla Frosting

Yield: approximately 4 cups

This recipe makes enough to frost and fill a 9" 2-layer cake.

1½ cup Florida Crystals
2 teaspoons agar
1½ tablespoons water
2 14-ounce blocks firm tofu
½ cup coconut oil
½ cup canola oil
¼ cup maple syrup
½ teaspoon salt
1 tablespoon vanilla extract

1. Put the Florida Crystals, agar and water into a small saucepan. Stir to dissolve and cook over medium heat until syrupy.

2. Blend together tofu, coconut oil, canola oil, maple syrup salt and, vanilla in a blender.

3. Add the syrupy mixture to the blender and blend until smooth. Refrigerate overnight.

Lemon Coconut Cake

Serves 8   **Yield: 1 9" layer cake**

Layers of cake are filled with tart lemon curd, frosted with our creamy vanilla coconut frosting and topped with coconut curls. This cake will make a beautiful addition to a garden party or anytime tea.

2 9" Vanilla Cakes, cooled (page 191)

Vanilla Coconut Frosting (page 194)

Lemon Curd Filling
2 cups apple cider
⅓ teaspoon turmeric
2 ½ tablespoons agar
1 cup rice syrup
¼ cup maple syrup
¾ cup lemon juice
¼ cup arrowroot
½ cup soymilk
4 teaspoons lemon zest
pinch salt
2 teaspoons vanilla extract

½ cup untoasted coconut flakes
1 cup toasted coconut

Make the Lemon Curd Filling:
1. In a medium saucepan, combine all the curd filling ingredients, and cook over medium-low heat, stirring until the mixture starts to thicken, about 10 minutes.

2. Chill for at least 4 hours, and then remix to a spreadable consistency.

To assemble the cake:
1. Level each cake by slicing off any rounded top. Then slice each cake in half horizontally to make 4 layers.

2. Spread ⅓ cup of lemon curd evenly onto one layer of the cake. Drop 3 tablespoons of the Vanilla Coconut Frosting onto the center of the layer.

3. Top with a second layer, and repeat step #2 with that and the third layer. Place the fourth layer on top.

4. Frost the outside of the cake with the remaining frosting. Sprinkle the coconut on the cake to finish.

Chef's Note:
The Vanilla Coconut Frosting should be refrigerated overnight, so be sure to make in advance.

Rainforest Crunch Cake   (photo page 129)

Serves 8   **Yield: 1 9" layer cake**

This moist, rich banana cake layered with chocolate ganache and fluffy Coconut frosting is coated with a delightful blend of sweet and crunchy Brazil nuts.

Vanilla coconut frosting
½ cup coconut oil
1 cup coconut milk
¼ cup maple syrup
1½ teaspoons sea salt
1½ cups organic sugar
1 tablespoon vanilla
2 14 ounce blocks extra-firm tofu, crumbled

2 9" Vanilla Layer Cakes (page 191), made with banana (instructions follow)

½ cup Chocolate Ganache (page 188)

Brazil Nut Crunch (recipe follows)

For the Vanilla Coconut Frosting:
1. In a blender, combine the coconut oil, coconut milk, maple syrup, sea salt, sugar and vanilla, and blend until mixed.

2. With the blender running on low speed, slowly add the crumbled tofu. Replace the lid and blend until smooth and glossy, scraping down the sides of the container a couple times.

3. Refrigerate overnight.

For the Banana Cake:
1. Prepare the vanilla cake with the addition of one large ripe mashed banana, mixed into the wet ingredients.

Chef's Tip:
ALWAYS turn off your blender before scraping the sides.

Brazil Nut Crunch

Brazil Nut Crunch
3 cups chopped Brazil nuts
½ cup maple syrup
½ cup Florida Crystals
½ teaspoon sea salt

For the Brazil Nut Crunch:
Preheat the oven to 375°.
Line a baking sheet with parchment paper and brush with a light coating of canola oil.

1. In a bowl, combine all the Brazil Nut Crunch ingredients and mix well until the sugar starts to dissolve.

2. Spread the mixture in the center of the prepared baking sheet and bake for 5 minutes. Turn the sheet around front to back and bake an additional 5 minutes.

3. Remove the sheet from the oven and let the Nut Crunch cool until hard & brittle.

4. Pull up the parchment and gently break up the brittle.

5. Transfer the brittle to a food processor and pulse to a rough gravel consistency. Set aside.

For the assembly:
1. Place one of the cooled layers on a plate, and spread the top with the chocolate ganache.

2. Carefully place the second layer on top of the first, checking to make sure they're lined up.

3. Frost the top and the sides of the cake with the vanilla coconut frosting.

4. Using your hand as a scoop, press the Brazil Nut Crunch into the frosted sides of the cake.

Tiramisu

Yield: 12 squares

Down to Earth's take on the traditional Italian classic is our most requested dessert. It's a rich and creamy perennial favorite.

1 recipe Vanilla Cake,
  baked in a jelly roll pan (page 191)

Vanilla Cream (page 192)

½ cup strong coffee or espresso
1 cup chopped chocolate chips

To assemble the Tiramisu:
1. Cut the cake in half width-wise and place one half in the bottom of a 9"x13" baking dish.

2. Moisten the cake with the strong coffee, then top with 1½ cups of the vanilla cream. Sprinkle with ½ cup of chocolate chips.

3. Place the other half of the cake on top, and then spread the remaining vanilla cream evenly over the cake. Sprinkle with the remaining chocolate.

4. Cover and refrigerate to let set, and then slice into squares and serve.

Luscious Chocolate Brownie Hazelnut Mousse Torte

Serves 8   Yield: 1 9" cake

This dessert dispels the myth that vegan and natural can't seem sinful.

Brownie Crust

Wet Ingredients
½ cup canola oil
½ cup maple syrup
¼ cup soymilk
1½ teaspoons vanilla extract

Dry Ingredients
1 cup unbleached flour
½ cup unsweetened cocoa powder
6 tablespoons Florida Crystals
¼ cup Sucanat
1 teaspoon baking powder
¾ teaspoon sea salt
½ cup chocolate chips

Chocolate Hazelnut Mousse

1 cup chocolate chips
1 12.3 ounce package silken Lite Tofu, firm or extra-firm
6 tablespoons Sucanat
½ teaspoon vanilla extract
pinch sea salt
1½ teaspoons chocolate extract
2 tablespoons hazelnut butter or any nut butter you like

Preheat oven to 350°.
Oil a 9" springform pan.

Make the Brownie Crust:
1. In a medium bowl, combine all the wet ingredients for the Brownie Crust and whisk to combine.

2. In a large bowl, combine all the dry ingredients for the Brownie Crust except the chocolate chips, and combine.

3. Fold the wet ingredients into the dry and gently combine. Fold in the chocolate chips.

4. Pour the batter into the oiled pan and bake for 20-25 minutes. Remove from the oven to cool.

Make the Hazelnut Mousse:
1. While the crust is cooling, melt the chocolate chips in the top part of a double boiler over boiling water.

2. Place the remaining Mousse ingredients in a blender or food processor, and process until smooth.

3. With the machine still running, add the melted chocolate.

4. Pour the mousse over the cooled brownie crust.

5. Return to the oven and bake for another 15-20 minutes or until the mousse pulls away from the sides of the pan.

6. Let the torte cool to the touch, cover, and refrigerate for 2 hours until completely firm.

Kit's Peach Skillet Cobbler

Serves 4-6

This is our editor Kit's vegan adaptation of a simple classic. The recipe works best with a 12" cast-iron skillet, but any oven-safe skillet or stove-to-oven 2 quart casserole will do.

3 tablespoons coconut oil
1 tablespoon apricot butter
    or apricot all-fruit preserves
4 pounds peaches, skinned, pitted, and
    sliced (about 8 medium peaches)
2 tablespoons Sucanat
1 tablespoon lemon juice
1 cup all-purpose flour
2 teaspoons baking powder
¾ cup Sucanat
¼ teaspoon salt
¾ cup non-dairy milk

Preheat the oven to 400°.

1. Melt the coconut oil in a 12" cast-iron skillet over medium-high heat and stir in the apricot butter or preserves.

2. Add the sliced peaches, Sucanat and lemon juice, and stir until the fruit softens a bit, roughly 3-5 minutes.

3. In a medium-sized bowl, mix together the flour, baking powder, Sucanat, and salt. Stir in the milk to make the batter.

4. Spoon the batter evenly over the fruit in the skillet.

5. Transfer the skillet to the oven and bake for 25 minutes, until the cobbler is golden brown. Serve warm.

For an extra treat, serve with a scoop of vanilla Soy Delicious. You can easily adapt this recipe for each season's fruit harvest. Simply replace the peach slices with 4-5 cups of berries, chopped rhubarb, sliced apples, pears, stone fruit or any combination of the above.

Chef's Tip:
To skin peaches, score the bottom of each peach with a shallow X. Drop the peaches into boiling water for 30 seconds, remove and transfer to a bowl of cold water. The skins will now easily peel right off.

Kid's Food

At Down to Earth, the importance food plays in the lives of children is a huge topic of discussion. Often we hear people say that children cannot survive on a vegan diet. In truth, it is convenience that often stands in the way of parents taking the extra steps to provide children with healthy food choices. We have proven the point by bringing up healthy vegan children in our families. One of the many great examples of healthy vegan kids we see is Ginjer, Gail's daughter, who is a strong, beautiful, and very smart child who is not lacking in any area of nutrition. She especially loves sea vegetables, a great source of minerals and vitamins.

We think that veganism is an evolutionary process for adults who choose it later in life, and it takes them time to get it right. Eating well takes determination because, sadly, our busy lives today don't allow us the needed time to take optimum care of ourselves. We can, however, set up a healthy foundation for our children. We can supply them with quality organic whole foods, fruits, vegetables, nuts, seeds, grains, beans and healthy fats that aid in the development of healthy minds and bodies. In the restaurant we offer simple foods for our little guests and they happily feast on vegetables, mashed potatoes, hummus, greens, beans and brown rice. Many children choose to eat smaller portions of the same foods their moms and dads are having.

In this chapter, we offer some creative tips for starting kids off on a healthful path and provide some recipes designed for them. We've also included a fun natural craft project to do with your children.

Children are our future and, in our opinion, we have the responsibility to teach them how to make this world more wonderful. An early understanding of how diet choices can be healthy, fun and delicious, while still impacting the earth in a positive way, is priceless knowledge for a child.

Raising Healthy Eaters

Allow your children to develop a relationship with their food. Make food shopping an enjoyable experience by talking to your children as you shop, telling them where the food comes from and what it can do for their bodies. If you have the opportunity, take your children to the local farmer's market and let them meet the farmers who grow their food. Give them the chance to smell the food, touch it and appreciate it. Allow them to choose – would you like an apple or a banana? But most of all, prepare the food for your child with love in your heart and try to eat smart. Children learn what they live.

Feeding kids on trips

These are some simple ideas for food to take on long or short trips with

- Dried fruit
- Fruit leather
- Juice boxes
- Small soymilk boxes
- Jars of baby food
- Trail mix
- Bottled water
- Steamed vegetables
- Crackers and pretzels
- Strips of toasted nori

For special treats, have a few natural lollypops tucked away.

Favorite Finger Foods

- O-shaped cereals
- Rice cakes
- Well cooked diced carrots
- Whole grain toast with the crusts removed
- French toast
- Tofu chunks
- Cooked peas
- Cooked pasta
- Avocado chunks
- Ripe pear slices
- Cooked apple slices

"Be Wary" Foods

The foods listed below can be a choking hazard for tiny throats, so keep a watch on your toddler with the following:

- Nuts
- Popcorn
- Seeds
- Celery
- Raw carrots
- Raw apples
- Grapes

Ants on a Log

Munch away on these little snacks.

celery ribs
nut butter of choice
raisins

Variation:
Blob on a Biscuit
Use crackers instead of celery and jam or jelly instead of raisins.

1. Cut the celery into three pieces and fill with the nut butter.

2. Top with raisins and enjoy.

Baby's Apricot Apple Purée

You can alter this recipe to your baby's tastes by substituting an equal amount of pears, peaches or just about any fruit, for the apples and/or apricots.

2 medium apples,
   peeled, cored and chopped
6 dried apricots, finely chopped
water, to cover

1. Place apples and apricots in a pan with just enough water to cover.

2. Bring to a boil, lower heat and simmer for 5 minutes.

3. Strain out the water and set aside.

4. Purée the mixture with a blender or hand blender, adding the reserved cooking water to thin if desired.

Baby's Hot Cereals

Serves 1

Banana Hot Cereal
1 tablespoon uncooked rolled oats
¾ cup water
1 small banana
2 teaspoons golden raisins

Prune Apple Hot Cereal
1 tablespoon uncooked rolled oats
¾ cup water
1 small apple, peeled, cored and chopped small
5 dried prunes, chopped

1. To prepare either hot cereal, place all ingredients in a small saucepan, cover and bring to a boil.

2. Reduce the heat and simmer gently for about 5 minutes, stirring occasionally to prevent sticking.

Chef Mommy's Tip:
You can use some breast milk to thin out the cereal if needed - your baby will love it even more.

Baby's Puréed Vegetables

Yield: 4 4 ounce jars
You can make this recipe with almost any vegetable, using these same instructions.

2 cups filtered water
pinch sea salt
1 large zucchini, cut in medium-sized pieces

1. In a small saucepan, bring the water and salt to a boil.

2. Put the zucchini in the boiling water and cook for 3 minutes.

3. Drain the zucchini, reserving a small amount of cooking water.

4. Using a blender, immersion blender or food processor, purée the zucchini. Thin with the reserved cooking water if desired.

Chef Mommy's Tip:
I love the Braun immersion blender with the attached cup. I made all my baby food with it.

Fresh Fruit Kabob

bananas, cut in bite-sized pieces
apples, cut in bite-sized pieces
green grapes
red grapes
pineapple chunks
melon, cubed
or any fruit in season
wooden skewers, 1 per person

Dipping Sauce
Yield: 1¼ cups
8 ounces plain soy yogurt
½ teaspoon cinnamon
1½ teaspoons vanilla extract
1 tablespoon maple syrup

shredded coconut meat or Granola
   (raw, page 117 or regular, page 176)
   for rolling

1. Skewer the fruits of choice onto the skewers

2. In a food processor, blend together the yogurt, cinnamon, vanilla extract, and maple syrup until smooth.

3. Pour the dip onto a plate. Spread the coconut or granola onto another plate.

4. Hold the kabob on each end and roll it in the dip and then into the granola or the coconut and serve

Seed Sprinkle

This is a perfect balance of omega oils, calcium, protein and zinc..

¼ cup hemp seeds
¼ cup sunflower seeds
¼ cup pumpkin seeds, roasted
¼ cup sesame seeds

1. In a coffee or spice grinder, grind each of the seeds separately into a fine meal, and then transfer to a medium bowl.

2. Mix well and store in an airtight container.

Sprinkle over oatmeal, yogurt, pasta or anything that will benefit from a nutty punch.

Super Power Fruit Shake

Serves 1
Just the thing to power your little Superhero!

1½ cups soy milk, rice milk or apple juice
1 small banana, sliced
¼ cup strawberries or blueberries
1 teaspoon flax oil
1 teaspoon spirulina seaweed

1. Blend all ingredients together in a blender until smooth.

Feel free to substitute your favorite fruit.

Toddler's Crunchy Salad Mix

Serves 2

1 beet, grated
1 apple, grated
1 carrot, grated
¾ cup thinly sliced green cabbage
2 teaspoons extra virgin olive oil
freshly squeezed juice of ½ lemon
1 teaspoon rice syrup or agave syrup
3 tablespoons sunflower seeds
½ cup dried cranberries

1. In a medium bowl, combine the beet, apple, carrot, and cabbage.

2. In a small bowl, whisk together the oil, lemon juice and rice or agave syrup together.

3. Pour over the salad and toss to mix.

4. Scatter sunflower seeds and cranberries over top and serve.

Trail Mix

Hungry for a snack? This one goes anywhere with you.

Granola (raw, page 117
  or regular, page 176)
nuts and seeds of choice
cereal rings
dried fruit of choice

Mix all items together and store in an airtight container. Serve often.

Play Clay

Yield: 1 cup non-edible clay

1 cup unbleached flour
½ teaspoon salt
2 tablespoons vegetable oil
2 tablespoons cream of tartar
1 cup water

For Coloring:
turmeric
spirulina seaweed
beet juice

1. In a medium saucepan cook the flour, salt, oil, tartar, and water over medium heat. Stir constantly until stiff.

2. Cool and knead out the lumps, while kneading in the food coloring, adding more as required.

3. Store in an airtight container.

Chef Mommy's Note:
Conventional food coloring is fine for this recipe, unless your child has a habit of munching on clay.

Acknowledgements

Our first thank you goes to our parents for giving us life. You've always inspired us to be better people and instilled a positive work ethic as well as true integrity. Thank you for seeing us through the challenging adolescent years and helping us to be more passionate human beings.

And thank you to our brothers and sisters for their support.

To Ginjer: for being such a good vegan angel and making the future of the world a beautiful reality.

Our beloved husbands James Doherty and Jason Silverio, for all the love, for supporting our dream, and for allowing us to be a brighter light to shine for the rest of the world. We love you so much and could never have done it without you.

Kit Libenschek for helping us get the book together. Her editing and computer mastery have been invaluable. Without her, our cookbook dream could not have become a reality.

Judith Weber for her invaluable support, wisdom, enthusiasm and expertise. This book would not have been what it is without her guidance.

Gail's Aunt Evelyn and Uncle Sy for their constant support and inspiration. Lacey's Nana for being an artistic cook and making food fun. Lacey's Grand Mary for making deliciously memorable chocolate cake, cookies, and caramel corn and Grandpa Ray for loving the sweets.

Everyone who has worked at Down to Earth: Gabrielle, Regina, Louis, Alexandria, Pat, Eli, Ben, Meghan, Ryan, Taj, Kenny and Adam have been so passionate and enthusiastic you inspired us everyday.

Elise, our schoolmate and friend for all her heartfelt work and deep love of all animals. Tiffany Romeo for coming to work so Gail could have the time to have spend with Ginjer when she first entered this world and being such a dedicated part of Down to Earth. All of our dedicated recipe testers (Sabrina, Stacy, Taj, Wendy, Bruce, Rosanne, Tami, Claire and Michelle) for spending many hours testing and tasting.

Doctor Tommy for turning so many people on to our food and helping us turn the lights on.

Natalie, so much love for hand-carving our gorgeous sign even though she never carved anything before and Azara for loving food at such a young age. Jose Gracias for doing such a wonderful job making the kitchen run smoothly and being with us through everything.

Trinity for helping us document and refine so many recipes.

Fran Waldmann for beautiful and creative design sense and being so "font"-tastic.

Acknowledgements (continued)

All the Tiffanys that have worked at Down to Earth and, especially to Tiffany Betts for being with us from the beginning and coming back to work when we really needed you. Kevin, our weekend warrior who went out of his way to cook us delicious vegan breakfasts before he came to work for us. Kate for her great organizational skills and computer savvy. Wendy Hollander, for her beautiful, soul-inspiring artwork that graces the walls of our restaurant.

Cheri Jiosne and Andre' Cholmondeley: You founded Second Nature Health Foods in Red Bank, NJ, and ran it so well for over a decade. You always had what we needed, gave us incredible support, and ordered food for us before we had an account with any of the major distributors.

Claudia Ansorge and Ansorge Unlimited for unwavering support, promotion and devotion.

Our first customers! John, Judy, Michael, Steve, Jim, and many more who loved our food, believed in our abilities and whose loyalty kept us going.

Our suppliers: Fresh Tofu (for the most delicious tofu on Earth); Ray's Seitan; and Albert's Organic Produce.

Hiranth Jaya Singh for helping us get this place open and getting us through those most chaotic first few days of service and for coming back years later to help with the food picture styling.

Chef Eric Tucker for his innovative style at San Francisco's Millennium restaurant—you elevated vegan cuisine.

Cindy, Clayton, Chris, Debbie, architect Steven Michael Peterson, and everyone at Metrovation.

Aunt Eva and Uncle Ron for the beautiful paintings and support. Aunt Abby for her enthusiasm.

Chef Laura Dardi, a dedicated and fabulous pastry chef and friend in the community who helped us in the formative stages of the restaurant and makes truly delicious cakes and food.

Finally, to Melissa for making our dream come true and letting Down to Earth and its love live on.

Resources

In this section we give you some sources for most of the ingredients in our recipes, as well as other interesting natural ingredients.

We have also included some of the important organizations that help the world and all its living creatures.

Resources

Vegan Food and Cooking Utensils:

Pangea
vegan products
1-800-340-1200
www.veganstore.com

Gold Mine Natural Food
macrobiotic, Asian foods, pantry staples, and hard to find grains and beans
1-800-475-3663
www.goldminenaturalfood.com

Omega Nutrition
organic oils
1-800-661-3529
www.omegaflo.com

Diamond Organics
organic produce, groceries, and beautiful gift baskets
1-888-674-2642
www.diamondorganics.com

Maine Coast Sea Vegetables
domestic and imported sea vegetables and products
1-207-565-2907
www.seaveg.com

Mountain Rose Herbs
organic herbs and spices
1-800-879-3337
www.mountainroseherbs.com

Whole Spice
organic herbs and spices
1-415-472-1750
www.wholespice.com

Eat Raw.Com
online resource for raw foods and products
1-866-432-8729
www.eatraw.com

Nature's First Food Online Store
raw food ingredients and lifestyle products
1-800-205-2350
www.Raw-food.com

Equal Exchange
Fair-Trade organic gourmet coffee, tea, and chocolate
1-774-776-7400
www.equalexchange.com

Eden Natural Foods
macrobiotic, natural, and Asian groceries
1-888-424-3336
www.edenfoods.com

Discount Juicers
Juicers, dehydrators, blenders, and water distillers
www.discountjuicers.com

Vegan Support

Vegan Outreach
Why Vegan is great vegan information
211 Indian Drive
Pittsburgh Pa 15238
1-412-968-0268
www.veganoutreach.org

The Sierra Club
www.sierraclub.org

The Green Party
www.greenparty.org

The Organic Pages
Guide to the national organic guidelines and standards
www.theorganicpages.com

Resources (continued)

PETA
People for ethical treatment of animals
www.peta.org

Farm Sanctuary
Organization for the protection of farm animals
www.farmsanctuary.org

Reading Materials

Diet for a New America — John Robbins
H.J. Kramer, 1998
An informative book on the impact the consumption of animal products has on our lives and on the earth. A life-changing read. Also on video.

Fast Food Nation — Eric Schlosser
Harper Perennial, 2002
An exposé look at the history of fast food and its progression.

Food and Healing — Annemarie Colbin
Ballantine Books, 1986
An informative and practical book on our personal and cultural relationships to food and healing.

The Safe Shoppers Bible
— David Steinman
Wiley, 1995

A Consumer Dictionary of Food Additives — Ruth Winter
Three Rivers Press, 2004

The Book of Whole Meals
— Annemarie Colbin
Ballantine Books, 1985
A look at creating balanced whole meals with philosophy and recipes.

Index

acknowledgements, 207
Adam's Ginger Oat Waffles, 166
Adam's Pink Lady Apple Salsa, 104
agar, 12
    in Lemon Coconut Cake, 193
    in Tiramisu, 196
    in Vanilla Frosting, 192
agave, 12
    in Almond Milk, 25
    in Avocado Ranch Dressing, 73
    in Hijiki Caviar, 85
    in Live Buckwheat Hempseed Granola Crunch, 117
    in Raw Apple Pie, 120
    in Raw Cream Whip Topping, 121
    in Spicy French Dressing, 74
Almond Milk, 25
    in French Toast, 165
almond(s):
    in Almond Milk, 25
    raw:
        in Curried Almond Pâté, 105
        in Nell's Coconut Rolls, 119
Ants on a Log, 201
appetizers, 45-58
Apple Crumb Muffins, 160
Apple Herb Stuffing, 136
apple juice:
    in Fruit Slushie, 154
    in Spirulina Rush, 158
    in Strawberry Sunrise, 158
    in Super Power Fruit Shake, 204
apple(s):
    in Adam's Pink Lady Apple Salsa, 104
    in Apple and Herb Bread Stuffing, 136
    in Apple Crumb Muffins, 160
    in Baby's Apricot Apple Purée, 201
    in Banana Ginger Chutney, 143
    in Fresh Fruit Kabobs, 203
    in Immune Booster, 155
    in Live Lemonade, 156
    in Prune Apple Hot Cereal, 202
    in Toddler's Crunchy Salad Mix, 204
applesauce:
    in Michelle's Blueberry Sour Cream Coffee Cake, 169
apricot(s):
    in Baby's Apricot Apple Purée, 201
arrowroot, 12
avocado:
    in Avocado Ranch Dressing, 73
    in Bliss Cup, 118
    in Quinoa Avocado Wrap with Tofu, 100
    in Raw Maki Hand Roll, 116
Baby's Apricot Apple Purée, 201
Baby's Hot Cereals, 202
Baby's Puréed Vegetables, 202
Baked Tofu, 26
    in Club Sandwich, 93
    in Crispy Wonton Packages, 49
    in Love Bowl, 139
balsamic vinegar, 12
bamboo shoot(s):
    in Thai Veggie Soup, 70
Banana Bread, 161
Banana Hot Cereal, 202
banana(s):
    in Banana Bread, 161
    in Banana Ginger Chutney, 143
    in Banana Hot Cereal, 202
    in Fresh Fruit Kabobs, 203
    in Fruit Slushie, 154
    in Rainforest Crunch Cake, 194
    in Spirulina Rush, 158
    in Strawberry Sunrise, 158
    in Super Power Fruit Shake, 204
Barbeque Sauce, 91
barley malt, 12
Basic Biscuits, 162
    in Tempeh Sausage and Gravy Biscuits, 163
basic equipment, 7-9
Basic Marinade, 26
basic technique(s), 9, 10
basics and sides. 21-43
basil:
    in Basil Lemongrass Sauce, 146
    in Gazpacho, 63
    in Pesto Sauce, 57
    in Roasted Tomato, Basil and Corn Salad, 88
    in White Bean Crepes, 148
BBQ Tofu Wrap, 90
bean(s) and legume(s):
  See also black bean(s), chickpea(s), lentil(s).
  about, 22; cooking chart, 22; soaking time, 22
  black-eyed peas, cooking, 22
    in Three Bean Chili, 66
  split pea(s) , cooking, 22
    in Split Pea Soup, 68
  white bean(s) , cooking, 22
    in Chickpea Socca, 134

Index (continued)

in White Bean Crepes, 148
beef broth, vegan substitute for: 19
beef, vegan substitute for: 19
beet(s):
    in Immune Booster, 155
    in Pickled Vegetables, 43
    in Spinach Salad with Beets and Pecans, 86
    in Toddler's Crunchy Salad Mix, 204
Black Bean Soup, 60
black bean(s):
cooking, 22
    in Three Bean Chili, 66
    in Black Bean Soup, 60
    in Love Bowl, 139
   fermented, 14
   in Scallion Pancakes with Plum and Dipping Sauces, 55
black olive(s) (see olive(s), black)
blanching, 9
Bliss Cup, 118
Blob on a Biscuit, 201
Blondies, 182
Blue Corn Hempeh, 132, 126
Blueberry Corn Muffins, 31
blueberry:
    in Blueberry Corn Muffins, 31
    in Fruit Slushie, 154
    in Lemon Blueberry Scones, 168
    in Michelle's Blueberry Sour Cream Coffee Cake, 169
    in Spirulina Rush, 158
    in Super Power Fruit Shake, 204
Brazil nuts:
    in Coconut Seitan, 141
    in Rainforest Crunch Cake, 194
   raw,
    in Raw Cheese Trio, 113
    in Raw Lemon Pie, 122
    in Raw Maki Hand Roll, 116
    in Sun-Dried Tomato Pâté, 107
Bread Sticks, 30
breakfast, 159-174
  about, 159
Broccoli Seitan Knishes, 92
broccoli:
    in Broccoli Seitan Knishes, 92
    in Dark Green Salad, 78
    in Quiche, 171
    in Raw Herb Vegetable Croquette, 114
    in Thai Veggie Soup, 70
brown rice (see rice, brown)

brown rice flour, 12
brown rice syrup:
    in Granola, 167
brown rice syrup, 13
Brownies, 183
buckwheat groats:
    in Live Buckwheat Hempseed Granola Crunch, 117
    in Live Pizza Crackers, 111
Bugs Bunny, 154
bulgur wheat, 13
  cooking: 23
    in Falafel, 96
butter, vegan substitute for: 19
cabbage:
  green:
    in Cole Slaw, 77
    in Dark Green Salad, 78
    in Gado Gado, 80
    in Sea Caesar/Cruelty-Free Caesar, 84
    in Toddler's Crunchy Salad Mix, 204
  napa
    in Crispy Wonton Packages, 49
  red:
    in Dark Green Salad, 78
    in Gado Gado, 80
    in Pickled Vegetables, 43
    in Sea Caesar/Cruelty-Free Caesar, 84
Cajun Spice Baked Potato Fries, 40
canola oil, 13
capers, 13
Caramelized Leeks, 29
Caramelized Onions, 29
    in Philly Seitan Sandwich, 95
carob, 13
    in Bliss Cup, 118
carrot juice:
    in Bugs Bunny, 154
    in Good Ol' Carrot, 155
carrot(s):
    in Chickpea Untuna Salad, 76
    in Cole Slaw, 77
    in Curried Red Lentil Soup, 62
    in Dark Green Salad, 78
    in Earth Burger, 94
    in Gado Gado, 80
    in Immune Booster, 155
    in Live Pizza Crackers, 111
    in Magic Cookies, 178
    in Mediterranean Lentil Soup, 64

Index (continued)

    in Pickled Vegetables, 44
    in Quiche, 171
    in Quinoa Salad, 82
    in Quinoa Vegetable Soup, 67
    in Raw Herb Vegetable Croquette, 114
    in Raw Maki Hand Roll, 116
    in Sea Caesar/Cruelty-Free Caesar, 84
    in Soba Noodles in Peanut Sauce, 83
    in Split Pea Soup, 68
    in Thai Veggie Soup, 70
    in Toddler's Crunchy Salad Mix, 204
    in Tofu Scramble, 174
    in Vegetable Stock, 24
    in Wild Rice Risotto Cakes, 150
Carson, Rachael, 4
Cashew Rice, 29
cashew(s):
    in Cashew Rice, 29
   raw,
    in Bliss Cup, 118
 in Raw Cashew Aioli, 115
    in Raw Cashew Cheese, 109
    in Raw Cheese Trio, 113
    in Raw Cream Whip Topping, 121
    in Raw Sour Cream, 110
celery:
    in Ants on a Log, 201
    in Apple and Herb Bread Stuffing, 136
    in Black Bean Soup, 60
    in Chickpea Untuna Salad, 76
    in Cole Slaw, 77
    in Mediterranean Lentil Soup, 64
    in Quinoa Vegetable Soup, 67
    in Sea Caesar, 84
    in Spicy French Dressing, 74
    in Split Pea Soup, 68
    in Vegetable Stock, 24
    in Wild Rice Risotto Cakes, 150
Cheesecake, 184
Chef Mommy's Tip(s),
    coloring Play Clay, 205
    thinning out cereal with breast milk, 202
    using immersion blender for baby food, 202
Chef's Tips:
    to adjust crispness of coleslaw, 77
    to avoid blender burn, 69
    to avoid Root Beer Float mess, 157
    to chiffonade, 78
    to clean leeks, 29

    to cut perfect crackers, 48
    to get cakes to release cleanly, 191
    to make an easy tahini casserole, 72
    to make extra fluffy pancakes, 173
    to make non-spackle mashed potatoes, 38
    to make quick smoothies, 154
    to mellow harsh red onions, 76
    to press tofu, 94
    to prevent papaya rollover, 170
    to rinse quinoa, 82
    to skin peaches, 198
chicken broth, vegan substitute for: 19
chicken, vegan substitute for: 19
chickpea flour, 13
    in Chickpea Socca, 134
Chickpea Socca, 134, 123
chickpea(s):
   cooking, 22
    in Chickpea Untuna Salad, 76
    in Falafel, 96
chiffonade, 9, 78
chipotle pepper(s) (see pepper(s), chipotle)
Chocolate Cake, 187
    in Chocolate Ganache Cake, 188
    in German Chocolate Cake, 189
    in Peanut Butter Chocolate Cake, 190
chocolate chips:
    in Blondies, 182
    in Chocolate Ganache, 188
    in Chocolate Sauce, 188
    in Hempseed Cookies, 176
    in Luscious Chocolate Brownie Hazelnut Mousse Torte, 197
    in Magic Cookies, 178
    in Tiramisu, 196
Chocolate Ganache Cake, 188
Chocolate Ganache, 188
    in Chocolate Ganache Cake, 188
    in Rainforest Crunch Cake, 194
Chocolate Sauce, 188
chutney, 13
cilantro:
    in Adam's Pink Lady Apple Salsa, 104
    in Gado Gado, 80
    in Gazpacho, 63
    in Live Nachos, 110
    in Live Salsa, 112
    in Quinoa Salad, 82
    in Seitan Satay, 144

Index (continued)

Cinnamon Buns, 164
Circulator, 154
Club Sandwich, 93
cocoa:
    in Brownies, 183
    in Chocolate Cake, 187
    in Luscious Chocolate Brownie Hazelnut Mousse Torte, 197
Coconut Seitan, 141
Coconut Squash Soup, 61
coconut:
    in Cashew Rice, 29
    in Coconut Seitan, 141
    in Fresh Fruit Kabobs, 203
    in Lemon Coconut Cake, 193
    in Magic Cookies, 178
    in Nell's Coconut Rolls, 119
    in Raw Lemon Pie, 122
    in Thai Coconut Tempeh Stix, 146
  milk: about, 13
    in Basil Lemongrass Sauce, 146
    in Coconut Squash Soup, 61
    in German Chocolate Cake, 189
    in Mashed Coconut Yams, 39
    in Nell's Coconut Rolls, 119
    in Peanut Butter Chocolate Cake, 190
    in Thai Veggie Soup, 70
    in Vanilla Coconut Frosting, 194
  oil: about, 13;
  toasted:
    in German Chocolate Cake, 189
    in Lemon Coconut Cake, 193
coffee:
    in Tiramisu, 196
Cole Slaw, 77
Collard Rolls, 46
collards (see greens, collards)
corn flour (see cornmeal)
corn:
    in Cornmeal Cakes, 47
    in Gazpacho, 63
    in Three Bean Chili, 66
    in Roasted Tomato, Basil and Corn Salad, 88
  baby:
    in Thai Veggie Soup, 70
Cornbread, 31
Cornmeal Cakes with Pico de Gallo, 47
cornmeal, 13
    in Blue Corn Hempeh, 132
    in Cornbread, 31
    in Cornmeal Cakes with Pico de Gallo, 47
    in Radiance's Fried Polenta Appetizer, 54
couscous, 13
Cranberry Orange Relish, 136
cream, vegan substitute for: 19
Creamy Chickpea Hummus & Oatmeal Garlic Crackers, 48
Crispy Wonton Packages, 49
Croutons, 75
    in Cruelty-Free Caesar, 84
Cruelty-Free Caesar, 84
Cucumber Salad, 97
cucumber:
    in Falafel's Cucumber Salad, 97
    in Gazpacho, 63
    in Greek Salad, 81
    in Gyros' Cucumber Dressing, 98
    in Quinoa Avocado Wrap with Tofu, 100
Curried Almond Pâté, 105
Curried Red Lentil Soup, 62
daikon, 14
Dark Green Salad, 78
date(s), 14
    in Bliss Cup, 118
    in Live Buckwheat Hempseed Granola Crunch, 117
    in Raw Apple Pie, 120
    in Raw Cream Whip Topping, 121
    in Raw Lemon Pie, 122
dehydrator recipes
dehydrator, 9
desserts, 175-198
  about, 175
drinks, juices and smoothies, 153-158
  about, 153
dulse, 14
Earth Burger, 94
egg replacer, 14
    in Hempseed Cookies, 176
Eggless Tofu Salad, 79
eggs, vegan substitute for: 19
entrées, 131-151
  about, 131
equipment, basic: 7-9
evaporated cane juice, 14
extra virgin olive oil, 14
Falafel, 96
fats and oils: 11 (see also specific types)
favorite toddler finger foods, 200
feeding kids on trips, 200

Index (continued)

fermented black beans (see black beans, fermented)
Flax Crackers, 106
    in Raw Cheese Trio, 113
flax oil, 14
    in Circulator, 154
    in Spirulina Rush, 158
    in Super Power Fruit Shake, 204
flax seeds, 14
    in Flax Crackers, 106
    in Live Nachos, 110
Florida Crystals, 14
flour, spelt:
    in Cheesecake, 184
    in Hempseed Cookies, 176
    in Jam Dot Cookies, 177
    in Maple Pecan Cookies, 179
    in Sugar Cookies, 181
flours, about, 14
foods to be wary of when feeding a toddler, 200
French Toast, 165
Fresh Fruit Kabob, 203
frosting(s):
    Chocolate Ganache, 188
    Coconut Frosting, 189
    Peanut Butter Frosting, 190
    Vanilla Coconut Frosting, 194
    Vanilla Frosting, 192
Fruit Sauce, 185
    in French Toast, 165
Fruit Slushie, 154
Gado Gado, 80, 128
garbanzo beans (see chickpeas)
garlic:
    in Barbeque Sauce, 91
    in Black Bean Soup, 60
    in Hijiki Caviar, 85
    in Immune Booster, 155
    in Live Salsa, 112
    in Tofu Scramble, 174
    in Wild Rice Risotto Cakes, 150
Gazpacho, 63
gelatin, vegan substitute for: 19
German Chocolate Cake, 189
Ginger Spice Cookies, 181
ginger, fresh:
    in Basil Lemongrass Sauce, 146
    in Circulator, 154
    in Hijiki Caviar, 85
    in Immune Booster, 155

    in Live Lemonade, 156
    in Marinated Tempeh, 28
    in Thai Veggie Soup, 70
ginger, pickled:
    in Peanut Sauce, 34
gluten flour, 14
    in Homemade Seitan, 27
goji berries, 15
Good Ol' Carrot, 155
grain coffee powder:
    in Blondies, 182
grains: (see also specific types)
   about, 23; cooking chart, 23
Granola, 167
    in Fresh Fruit Kabobs, 203
    in Papaya Delight, 170
    in Strawberry Sunrise, 158
    in Trail Mix, 205
grapes:
    in Fresh Fruit Kabobs, 203
Greek Salad, 81
greens:
    in Immune Booster, 155
    in Live Pizza Crackers, 111
  collards:
    in Collard Rolls, 46
  kale:
    in Sautéed Greens, 42
Grilled Zucchini Rollatini, 50
Gyro Bread, 99
Gyros, 98
hemp seeds, 15
    in Banana Bread, 161
    in Blue Corn Hempeh, 132
    in Granola, 167
    in Hempseed Cookies, 176
    in Live Buckwheat Hempseed Granola Crunch, 117
    in Seed Sprinkle, 203
    in Spirulina Rush, 158
Hempseed Cookies, 176
Herbed Tofu Loaf, 137
Hijiki Caviar, 85
    in Sea Caesar, 84
Hijiki Sea Cakes, 135
hijiki, 15
    in Hijiki Caviar, 85
    in Hijiki Sea Cakes, 135
hiziki (see hijiki)
Homemade Seitan, 27

Index (continued)

House Marinara, 32
    in Chickpea Socca, 134
    in Radiance's Fried Polenta Appetizer, 54
    in Vegetable Lasagna, 147
    in Wheatball Sub, 102
Hummus, 48
Immune Booster, 155
Jalapeño(es):
    in Adam's Pink Lady Apple Salsa, 104
    in Cornbread, 31
    in Live Nachos, 110
Jam Dot Cookies, 177
jasmine rice (see rice, jasmine)
kale (see greens, kale)
ketchup:
    in Spicy French Dressing, 74
Kevin's Tofu Murphy, 138
kid's food, 199-205
  about, 199
Kit's Peach Skillet Cobbler, 198
knives, 7
kombu, 15
    in cooking beans, 22
kudzu (see kuzu)
kuzu, 15
    in Mushroom Gravy, 33
Leaf Wraps, 107, 125
leek(s):
  cleaning, 29
    in Caramelized Leeks, 29
    in Leek and Red Pepper Sauce, 164
    in Potato Leek Soup, 65
Lemon Blueberry Scones, 168
Lemon Coconut Cake, 193
lemon(s):
    in Circulator, 154
    in Immune Booster, 155
    in Lemon Blueberry Scones, 168
    in Lemon Coconut Cake, 193
    in Live Lemonade, 156
lemongrass:
    in Basil Lemongrass Sauce, 146
    in Thai Veggie Soup, 70
lentil(s):
  cooking, 22
    in Mediterranean Lentil Soup, 64
  red:
    in Curried Red Lentil Soup, 62
Lidzbarski, Ed, 1

lime(s):
    in Adam's Pink Lady Apple Salsa, 104
    in Banana Ginger Chutney, 143
  juice:
    in Live Salsa, 112
Live Buckwheat Hempseed Granola Crunch, 117
    in Papaya Delight, 170
    in Strawberry Sunrise, 158
    in Trail Mix, 205
live foods, 103-122
Live Lasagna, 108
Live Lemonade, 156
Live Nachos, 110
Live Pizza Crackers, 111, 124
Live Salsa, 112
    in Live Nachos, 110
    in Potato Skins, 53
Live Tomato Sauce, 109
    in Live Lasagna, 108
Love Bowl, 139
Luscious Chocolate Brownie Hazelnut Mousse Torte, 197
Maegan's Heartburn Helper, 156
Magic Cookies, 178
mango:
    in Coconut Seitan, 141
Maple Miso Dressing, 72
Maple Pecan Cookies, 179
maple syrup, 15
    in Blondies, 182
    in Cheesecake, 184
    in Chocolate Cake, 187
    in Granola, 167
    in Jam Dot Cookies, 177
    in Luscious Chocolate Brownie Hazelnut Mousse Torte, 197
    in Maple Miso Dressing, 72
    in Maple Pecan Cookies, 179
    in Spicy Maple Sauce, 58
Marinated Stuffed Mushrooms, 51
Marinated Tempeh, 28
    in Blue Corn Hempeh, 132
    in Love Bowl, 139
    in Marinated Stuffed Mushrooms, 51
    in Tempeh Sausage and Gravy Biscuits, 163
    in Thai Coconut Tempeh Stix, 146
    in Three Bean Chili, 66
Mashed Coconut Yams, 39
Mashed Potatoes, 38
    in Blue Corn Hempeh, 132

Index (continued)

mayonnaise, vegan substitute for: 19
Mediterranean Lentil Soup, 64
melon:
    in Fresh Fruit Kabobs, 203
Michelle's Blueberry Sour Cream Coffee Cake, 169
millet, 15
  cooking, 23
mirin, 15
miso, 15
  in Maple Miso Dressing, 72
  in Raw Maki Hand Roll, 116
  in Spicy French Dressing, 74
  in Tofu Cheese: 36
Mushroom Gravy, 33
  in Blue Corn Hempeh, 132
  in Love Bowl, 139
mushrooms:
  button:
    in Marinated Stuffed Mushrooms, 51
    in Mushroom Gravy, 33
  Portobello:
    in Kevin's Tofu Murphy, 138
    in Live Lasagna, 108
    in Pan Grilled Mushroom Tapenade, 52
    in Tortilla Torte, 57
  shiitake, 16
    in Crispy Wonton Packages, 49
    in Pan Grilled Mushroom Tapenade, 52
nama shoyu, 15
  in Curried Almond Pâté, 105
nectarine(s):
  in Adam's Ginger Oat Waffles, 166
Nell's Coconut Rolls, 119
noodles,
  lasagna,
    in Vegetable Lasagna, 147
  soba,
    in Soba Noodles in Peanut Sauce, 83
nori, 16
  in Raw Maki Hand Roll, 116
  in Sea Caesar, 84
nut butter:
  in Ants on a Log, 201
  in Blob on a Biscuit, 201
  in Luscious Chocolate Brownie Hazelnut Mousse Torte, 197
nutritional yeast, 16
  in Avocado Ranch Dressing, 73
  in Chickpea Untuna Salad, 76
  in Eggless Tofu Salad, 79
  in Flax Crackers, 106
  in French Toast, 165
  in Herbed Tofu Loaf, 137
  in Live Nachos, 110
  in Live Tomato Sauce, 109
  in Nutro Cheese, 35
  in Quiche, 171
  in Raw Cashew Cheese, 109
  in Raw Cheese Trio, 113
  in Sprinkle Cheese, 36
  in Tempeh Sausage and Gravy Biscuits, 163
  in Tofu Nuggets, 87
  in Tofu Parmesan Sandwich, 101
  in Tofu Scramble, 174
  in Tortilla Torte, 57
Nutro Cheese, 35
  in Philly Seitan Sandwich, 95
Oatmeal Garlic Crackers, 48
Oatmeal Raisin Cookies, 180
oats, 16
  in Adam's Ginger Oat Waffles, 166
  in Apple Crumb Muffins, 160
  in Baby's Hot Cereals, 202
  in Cheesecake, 184
  in Earth Burger, 94
  in Granola, 167
  in Jam Dot Cookies, 177
  in Magic Cookies, 178
  in Maple Pecan Cookies, 179
  in Oatmeal Garlic Crackers, 48
  in Oatmeal Raisin Cookies, 180
  in Pumpkin Cheesecake, 186
olive(s):
  black:
    in Cruelty-Free Caesar, 84
  Greek:
    in Greek Salad, 81
onion(s):
  in Barbeque Sauce, 91
  in Caramelized Onions, 29
  in Hijiki Caviar, 85
  in Kevin's Tofu Murphy, 138
  in Live Salsa, 112
  in Pickled Vegetables, 43
  in Split Pea Soup, 68
  in Three Bean Chili, 66
  in Tofu Cheese, 36
  in Vegetable Stock, 24

Index (continued)

    in Wheatball Sub, 102
  red,
    in Gazpacho, 63
    in Greek Salad, 81
    in Live Salsa, 112
    in Tofu Scramble, 174
orange juice:
  in Quinoa Avocado Wrap with Tofu, 100
organic produce, importance of; 4-5
Papaya Delight, 170
papaya:
  in Papaya Delight, 170
parsley:
  in Pesto Sauce, 57
peach(es):
  in Kit's Peach Skillet Cobbler, 198
Peanut Butter and Jam Cookies, 178
Peanut Butter Cake, 190
peanut butter:
  in Blondies, 182
in Gado Gado, 80
  in Peanut Butter Chocolate Cake, 190
  in Peanut Sauce, 34
Peanut Sauce, 34
  in Love Bowl, 139
  in Seitan Satay, 144
  in Soba Noodles in Peanut Sauce, 83
peanut(s):
  in Gado Gado, 80
  in Jam Dot Cookies, 177
pecan(s):
  in Cheesecake, 184
  in German Chocolate Cake, 189
  in Granola, 167
  in Magic Cookies, 178
  in Maple Pecan Cookies, 179
  in Pumpkin Cheesecake, 186
  in Spinach Salad with Beets and Pecans, 86
  in Zucchini Pecan Mini Pancakes, 58
  raw:
    in Raw Cheese Trio, 113
pepper(s):
  Anaheim chili:
    in Banana Ginger Chutney, 143
  ancho chili:
    in Barbeque Sauce, 91
  cherry:
    in Kevin's Tofu Murphy, 138
  chipotle:

    in Black Bean Soup, 60
    in Sweet Potato Tomato Chipotle Soup, 69
  green bell:
    in Kevin's Tofu Murphy, 138
    in Three Bean Chili, 66
  red bell:
    in Gazpacho, 63
    in Kevin's Tofu Murphy, 138
    in Leek and Red Pepper Sauce, 151
    in Quinoa Salad, 82
    in Tofu Scramble, 174
  roasted red:
    in Coconut Seitan, 141
  yellow bell:
    in Kevin's Tofu Murphy, 138
Philly Seitan Sandwich, 95
phyllo dough, 16
Pickled Vegetables, 43
pine nut(s):
  in Adam's Ginger Oat Waffles, 166
pineapple:
  fresh:
    in Coconut Seitan, 141
    in Fresh Fruit Kabobs, 203
  rings, dried:
in Raw Lemon Pie, 122
pinto beans,:
  cooking, 22
  in Three Bean Chili, 66
Pizza, 140
Play Clay, 205
plum preserves:
  in Scallion Pancakes with Plum and Dipping Sauces, 55
Potato Leek Soup with Lemon and Dill, 65
Potato Skins, 53
potato(es):
  in Broccoli Seitan Knishes, 92
  in Cajun Spice Baked Potato Fries, 40
  in Mashed Potatoes, 38
  in Potato Leek Soup, 65
  in Potato Skins, 53
  in Samosas, 142
  in Split Pea Soup, 68
  sweet:
    in Collard Rolls, 46
    in Curried Red Lentil Soup, 62
  Yukon Gold,
    in Kevin's Tofu Murphy, 138
pots and pans, 7

Index (continued)

Prune Apple Hot Cereal, 202
Pumpkin Cheesecake, 186
pumpkin Purée:
    in Pumpkin Cheesecake, 186
pumpkin seed(s):
    in Granola, 167
    in Seed Sprinkle, 203
   raw:
    in Dark Green Salad, 78
    in Live Pizza Crackers, 111
    in Raw Cheese Trio, 113
    in Raw Herb Vegetable Croquette, 114
    in Raw Maki Hand Roll, 116
Quiche, 171
Quinoa Avocado Wrap, 100
Quinoa Salad, 82
Quinoa Vegetable Soup, 67
quinoa, 16
  cooking, 23
  washing: 82
    in Collard Rolls, 46
    in Quinoa Avocado Wrap with Tofu, 100
    in Quinoa Salad, 82
    in Quinoa Vegetable Soup, 67
Radiance's Fried Polenta Appetizer, 54
Rainforest Crunch Cake, 194, 129
raisin(s):
    in Ants on a Log, 201
    in Banana Ginger Chutney, 143
    in Oatmeal Raisin Cookies, 180
    in Raw Apple Pie, 120
  golden,
    in Banana Hot Cereal, 202
raising healthy eaters, 200
raspberry fruit spread:
    in Jam Dot Cookies, 177
raspberry:
    in Bliss Cup, 118
Raw Apple Pie, 120
Raw Cashew Cheese, 109
    in Live Lasagna, 108
    in Live Pizza Crackers, 111
Raw Cheese Trio, 113
Raw Cream Whip Topping, 121
    in Raw Apple Pie, 120
Raw Lemon Pie, 122
Raw Maki Hand Roll, 116, 124
Raw Sour Cream, 110
Raw Vegetable Herb Croquette, 114

recipe conversion ideas: 19
resources, 211
rice malt (see brown rice syrup)
rice milk, 16
    in Strawberry Sunrise, 158
    in Super Power Fruit Shake, 204
rice vinegar, 16
rice, brown:
  cooking, 23
    in Earth Burger, 94
    in Love Bowl, 139
rice, jasmine:
  cooking (long grain), 23
    in Cashew Rice, 29
rice, wild:
    in Wild Rice Risotto Cakes, 150
Roasted Tomato, Basil and Corn Salad, 88
Roasted Yams, 39
romaine lettuce:
    in BBQ Tofu Wrap, 90
    in Gado Gado, 80
    in Greek Salad, 81
    in Gyros, 98
    in Leaf Wraps, 107
    in Sea Caesar/Cruelty-Free Caesar, 84
Root Beer Float, 157, 129
salad dressings:
  Avocado Ranch Dressing, 73
  Caesar Dressing, 84
  Fennel Apple Dressing, 73
  Fresh Herb Vinaigrette, 75
  Gado Gado Dressing, 80
  Greek Dressing, 81
  Maple Miso Dressing, 72
  Smokey Toasted Sesame Dressing, 74
Spicy French Dressing, 74
  Tangy Tahini Dressing, 72
salads, 71-88
  about, 71
Samosas, 142
sandwiches and wraps, 89-102
sauces:
  Aioli, in Marinated Stuffed Mushrooms, 51
  Barbeque Sauce, in BBQ Tofu Wrap, 91
  Basil "Butter", in White Bean Crepes, 148
  Basil Lemongrass Sauce, in Thai Coconut Tempeh Stix, 146
  Cool Ranch Dressing, in Tofu Hot Wings, 56
  Herb Gravy, in Tempeh Sausage and Gravy Biscuits, 163
  Hot Wing Sauce, in Tofu Hot Wings, 56

Index (continued)

Leek and Red Pepper Sauce, in Wild Rice Risotto Cakes, 150
Lentil Sauce, in Collard Rolls, 46
Live Tomato Sauce, in Live Lasagna, 109
Maple Mustard Sauce, in Southern Style Seitan, 145
Mushroom Gravy, 33
Peanut Sauce, 34
Pesto Sauce, in Tortilla Torte, 57
Pico de Gallo, in Cornmeal Cakes 47
Plum Sauce, in Scallion Pancakes, 55
Spicy Maple Sauce, in Zucchini Pecan Mini Pancakes, 58
Tahini Sauce, in Falafel, 97
Tamarind Sauce, in Samosas, 143
Tartar Sauce, in Hijiki Sea Cakes, 135
Yellow Mustard Sauce, in Blue Corn Hempeh, 132
sauté, 9
Sautéed Greens, 42
    in Chickpea Socca, 134
    in Philly Seitan Sandwich, 95
    in Wheatball Sub, 102
Scallion Pancakes with Plum and Dipping Sauces, 55
scallion(s):
    in Live Salsa, 112
    in Scallion Pancakes, 55
    in Soba Noodles with Peanut Sauce, 83
Sea Caesar, 84
sea salt, 16
sea vegetables: (see also specific types)
    about, 11
seaweed (see sea vegetables)
Seed Sprinkle, 203
Seitan Satay, 144, 128
seitan, 16
    in Broccoli Seitan Knishes, 92
    in Coconut Seitan, 141
    in Gyros, 98
    in Philly Seitan Sandwich, 95
    in Seitan Satay, 144
    in Southern Style Seitan, 145
    in Wheatball Sub, 102
sesame butter (see tahini)
sesame seeds:
    in Seed Sprinkle, 203
    in Sesame Yams, 41
    in Smokey Toasted Sesame Dressing, 74
    raw:
    in Flax Crackers, 106
    in Live Nachos, 110
    in Live Pizza Crackers, 111
Sesame Yams, 41

shiitake mushroom(s) (see mushroom(s), shiitake)
Soba Noodles in Peanut Sauce, 83
soups, 59-70
    about, 59
Southern Style Seitan, 145
soy ice cream:
    in Soy Shake, 157
    vanilla:
    in Bugs Bunny, 154
    in Root Beer Float, 157
Soy Shake, 157
soy yogurt:
    in Cucumber Salad, 97
    in Fresh Fruit Kabobs, 203
    in Papaya Delight, 170
spelt flour (see flour, spelt)
spice blends, 20
Spike, 17
Spinach Salad with Beets and Pecans, 86
spinach:
    in Live Lasagna, 108
    in Quinoa Vegetable Soup, 67
    in Raw Maki Hand Roll, 116
    in Spinach Salad with Beets and Pecans, 86
    in Tortilla Torte, 57
    in Vegetable Lasagna, 147
    in White Bean Crepes, 148
Spirulina Rush, 158
spirulina, 17
    in Spirulina Rush, 158
    in Super Power Fruit Shake, 204
Split Pea Soup, 68
Sprinkle Cheese, 36
    in Cruelty-Free Caesar, 84
    in Leaf Wraps, 107
    in Live Lasagna, 108
    in Live Pizza Crackers, 111
    in Tofu Parmesan Sandwich, 101
    in Wheatball Sub, 102
squash, butternut:
    in Coconut Squash Soup, 61
squash, summer:
    in Dark Green Salad, 78
    in Live Lasagna, 108
    in Quinoa Vegetable Soup, 67
Strawberry Sunrise, 158
strawberry:
    in Fruit Slushie, 154
    in Strawberry Sunrise, 158

Index (continued)

    in Super Power Fruit Shake, 204
Sucanat, 17
Sugar Cookies, 181
Sun-Dried Tomato Pâté, 107
    in Leaf Wraps, 107
sun-dried tomato(es) (see tomato(es), sun-dried)
sunflower seeds:
    in Earth Burger, 94
    in Granola, 167
    in Oatmeal Garlic Crackers, 48
    in Seed Sprinkle, 203
   raw:
    in Dark Green Salad, 78
    in Live Buckwheat Hempseed Granola Crunch, 117
    in Live Nachos, 110
    in Live Pizza Crackers, 111
    in Raw Herb Vegetable Croquette, 114
    in Sun-Dried Tomato Pâté, 107
Super Power Fruit Shake, 204
Sweet Potato Tomato Chipotle Soup, 69
sweet potato(es) (see potato(es), sweet)
sweeteners, 11
Tahini Sauce, 97
tahini, 17
    easy Tahini Casserole, 72
    in Blondies, 182
    in Tahini Sauce,
    in Tangy Tahini Dressing, 72
tamari, 17
    in Basic Marinade, 26
    in Marinated Tempeh, 28
tamarind paste, 17
    in Gado Gado, 80
    in Tamarind Sauce, 143
Tangy Tahini Dressing, 72
Tempeh Bacun, 172
    in Club Sandwich, 93
Tempeh Sausage and Gravy Biscuits, 163
tempeh, 17
    in Marinated Tempeh, 28
    in Tempeh Bacun, 172
    in White Bean Crepes, 148
texturized vegetable protein, whole foods substitute for: 19
Thai Coconut Tempeh Stix, 146
Thai Veggie Soup, 70
Three Bean Chili, 66
    in Potato Skins, 53
Tiffany's Pancakes, 173, 127
Tiramisu, 196

Toddler's Crunchy Salad Mix, 204
Tofu Cheese, 36
in Grilled Zucchini Rollatini, 50
    in Tortilla Torte, 57
    in Vegetable Lasagna, 147
Tofu Nuggets, 87
Tofu Parmesan Sandwich, 101
Tofu Scramble, 174
Tofu Sour Cream, 37
    in Cornmeal Cakes, 47
    in Potato Skins, 53
tofu, 17
    pressing, 94
    in Baked Tofu, 26
    in BBQ Tofu Wrap, 90
    in Cheesecake, 184
    in Earth Burger, 94
    in Eggless Tofu Salad, 79
    in Gado Gado, 80
    in Greek Salad, 81
    in Gyros' Cucumber Dressing, 98
    in Herbed Tofu Loaf, 137
    in Hijiki Sea Cakes, 135
    in Kevin's Tofu Murphy, 138
    in Luscious Chocolate Brownie Hazelnut Mousse Torte, 197
    in Peanut Butter Chocolate Cake, 190
    in Pumpkin Cheesecake, 186
    in Quiche, 171
    in Quinoa Avocado Wrap with Tofu, 100
    in Rainforest Crunch Cake, 194
    in Tiramisu, 196
    in Tofu Cheese, 36
    in Tofu Hot Wings, 56
    in Tofu Nuggets, 87
    in Tofu Parmesan Sandwich, 101
    in Tofu Scramble, 174
    in Tofu Sour Cream, 37
    in Vanilla Frosting, 192
tomato paste:
    in Barbeque Sauce, 91
Tomato Pudding, 133
    in Blue Corn Hempeh, 132
tomato sauce:
    in Mediterranean Lentil Soup, 64
    in Wheatball Sub, 102
tomato(es):
    in BBQ Tofu Wrap, 90
    in Black Bean Soup, 60

Index (continued)

in Gazpacho, 63
in Greek Salad, 81
in Gyros, 98
in House Marinara, 32
in Live Salsa, 112
in Live Tomato Sauce, 109
in Pico de Gallo, 47
in Quinoa Avocado Wrap with Tofu, 100
in Roasted Tomato, Basil and Corn Salad, 88
in Sweet Potato Tomato Chipotle Soup, 69
in Three Bean Chili, 66
  sun-dried, 17
in Cruelty-Free Caesar, 84
in Dark Green Salad, 78
in Grilled Zucchini Rollatini, 50
in Live Pizza Crackers, 111
in Live Tomato Sauce, 109
in Raw Cheese Trio, 113
in Sun-Dried Tomato Pâté, 107
Tortilla Torte with Creamy Pumpkin Seed Pesto, 57
tortilla(s):
  in BBQ Tofu Wrap, 90
  in Quinoa Avocado Wrap with Tofu, 100
  in Samosas, 142
  in Tortilla Torte, 57
Trail Mix, 205
udon (see noodles, udon)
umeboshi paste, 17
  in Raw Cheese Trio, 113
  in Tofu Cheese, 36
umeboshi vinegar
Vanilla Cake, 191
  in Lemon Coconut Cake, 193
  in Rainforest Crunch Cake, 194
  in Tiramisu, 196
Vanilla Coconut Frosting, 194
  in Lemon Coconut Cake, 193
  in Rainforest Crunch Cake, 194
Vanilla Frosting, 192
vegan mozzarella:
  in Tofu Parmesan Sandwich, 101
Vegetable Lasagna, 147
Vegetable Stock, 24
vinegar, 11 (see also specific types)
vital wheat gluten (see gluten flour)
wakame, 18
walnut(s):
  in Lemon Blueberry Scones, 168
  in Oatmeal Raisin Cookies, 180

  raw:
    in Raw Herb Vegetable Croquette, 114
    in Sprinkle Cheese, 36
wasabi: 18
  in Raw Maki Hand Roll, 116
Wheatball Sub (aka Hoagie, Grinder, Hero), 102
White Bean Crêpes with Balsamic Grilled Tempeh, 148
Wild Rice Risotto Cakes, 150
yam(s):
  in Mashed Coconut Yams, 39
  in Quinoa Vegetable Soup, 67
  in Roasted Yams, 39
  in Sesame Yams, 41
  in Sweet Potato Tomato Chipotle Soup, 69
  in Vegetable Lasagna, 147
Zucchini Pecan Mini Pancakes, 58
zucchini:
  in Baby's Puréed Vegetables, 202
  in Grilled Zucchini Rollatini, 50
  in Live Lasagna, 108
  in Live Pizza Crackers, 111
  in Quiche, 171
  in Tofu Scramble, 174
  in Zucchini Pecan Mini Pancakes, 58